TOKYO PINK GUIDE

> **WARNING:** This book was researched by the author at his own risk. Neither the author nor the publisher will take responsibility for any misfortune met by persons who venture into the institutions or who participate in the activities described in this volume.

TOKYO PINK GUIDE

Steven Langhorne Clemens

Everything you want to know
about Tokyo's sexy pleasure spots...
What, where, and how much!

Illustrated by Paul Nowak

Published by YENBOOKS
Editorial offices at
2-6, Suido 1-chome, Bunkyo-ku, Tokyo 112, Japan

© 1993 YENBOOKS

LCC Card No. 93-60527
ISBN 0-8048-1915-7

First edition, 1993
Third printing, 1997

Printed in Singapore

CONTENTS

▼▼▼▼▼▼▼▼▼▼▼▼▼▼▼▼▼▼▼▼▼▼▼▼▼▼▼▼▼

ACKNOWLEDGMENTS

▼▼▼▼▼▼▼▼▼▼▼▼▼▼▼▼▼▼▼▼▼▼▼▼▼▼▼▼▼

It's amazing just how many friends you make when word gets around that you are doing a book about the raunchier aspects of night life in Tokyo. Most newfound pals desperately asked to accompany me during the field research, others seriously begged for fortnightly debriefings. No one offered to help pick up the tab.

Along the way to handing in this manuscript were a few friends indeed. Many would rather not see their names published here for reasons that will become obvious as you peruse the chapters, but let me assure the reader that those inscribed here for posterity mostly engaged in assisting with the more mundane but nonetheless extremely valuable tasks of helping with translations, proofreading, and passing along valuable contacts.

Nadja Kelman spent hours on the phone tracking down leads as her Japanese is much superior to mine. Her polite and fluent Osaka-accented voice helped open many doors. Kim Aylward journeyed into some venues where the doors were closed to me to get the woman's perspective on the host bars. Ms. Ishimura, Ms.

Yamazaki, Mr. Fujii, Mr. Fujita, and many other Japanese friends were always there when I needed them for advice and assistance. A debt of gratitude is due to colleague E. Vincent Sherry for understanding why I was a bit bleary-eyed during the times we were working together on more highbrow journalistic endeavors.

Thanks to a couple of broadcasting legends, the two Bruces, Mac Donnel and Dunning, who in large part are responsible for making it possible for me to remain in Japan. Fellow authors or journalists Eric Sedensky, Mike Millard, Jude Brand, Mark Schreiber, Boye Lafayette De Mente, Peter Hadfield, Bob Collins, and Philip Sandoz gave invaluable advice about the nuts and bolts of the publishing world if not the water trade.

My editor deserves a large share of the praise, but not the condemnation, for making sure this book made it to the galleys. Disc jockey and backgammon buddy Robert Susumu-Harris was kind enough to give the book some pre-publication publicity on J-Wave radio. Another veteran Asia hand, we'll call Buffalo Bill, went above and beyond the call of duty in making the S&M chapter possible. His scariest journalistic assignment will undoubtedly be the subject of Press Club gossip for years to come.

Although this is perhaps one of its more dubious accolades during its nearly 50 years, the Foreign Correspondents' Club of Japan also proved for this author to be an invaluable hangout for meeting contacts and its staff made the goings so much easier as it has for many budding and veteran Tokyo foreign scribes.

Finally, a hearty toast to an antecedent by the name of Samuel Langhorne Clemens whose spirit hopefully permeates this undertaking.

INTRODUCTION

▼▼▼▼▼▼▼▼▼▼▼▼▼▼▼▼▼▼▼▼▼▼▼▼▼▼▼▼▼

History of Sex in Japan

My deflowering in the pink world of Japan came in 1981, when a group of bank employees from Yamagata stationed in Tokyo asked me to join them on an outing to a *nō-pan kissa* near Kanda. Never one to turn down an invitation to carouse, I accepted while trying to figure just what kind of place we were heading to. Still struggling to learn Japanese, I knew that *kissa* was short for *kissaten*, the word for coffee shop. But what was so special about a coffee house that made a point of not serving bread? (*Pan* is the Japanese word for bread, taken from the Portuguese.)

On our entrance to the establishment, I noticed that bread was not the only thing missing. All of the waitresses were topless. Despite being over the legal age, it was my first time in such an environment (except for brief glimpses of the breasts of showgirls on the casino showroom stages of my hometown of Las Vegas) and I immediately began worrying about what the protocol was. What would I do if the waitress asked me if I wanted something besides a drink? While enmeshed in my angst I tried not to stare at the bevy of breasts prancing about the *kissaten*.

My bank salarymen buddies were carrying on as if there was nothing unusual. None of them appeared to be sneaking glances at the trio of topless young women.

A couple of *mizuwari* (whiskey and water on the rocks) later, I asked Toshi from the foreign currency department why the place was referred to as a *"nō-pan kissa."* "Steve-san, you don't know?" he chided me as if I had just arrived from Narita Airport. *"Pan* is Japanese-English for panty. *Nō-pan* is no panty."

The waitresses were wearing short skirts so it seemed academic that they were naked below the only piece of clothing in which they were attired. I explained this to Toshi. "They're not wearing panty. Didn't you notice?" He pointed to the mirror on the floor in front of the sofa we were all sitting on. Now I realized why all the guys were glancing down every time one of the girls approached us. The next time one of the waitresses strolled over I glanced down too and discovered truth in advertising.

During the remainder of my initial two-year stay in Japan I only once more ventured into a *nō-pan kissa* where customers were automatically served a poor quality of tea and there was nothing else on the menu. I left after about five minutes. I just didn't get it, I told myself. The experience didn't seem very erotic, a bit like those topless carwashes popping up in Florida, a novelty and little else.

When I returned to Japan in 1990 I was reintroduced to the "pink" world, as it is called here. I was nearly ten years older than when I had lived here before, divorced, and more able just to relax and have a good time out with the boys watching women do their stuff on the stages of Kabukicho. It was also, I discovered, a great way to engage in that all-important art of *nemawashii*—root binding. In Japanese business, it seems that men who have spent an evening together staring at breasts can do business. It was all a part of that macho buddy stuff that my feminist friends had cast so much scorn upon.

It is, of course, not unfair to label Japan a sexist country. In Japanese society, a woman's place is still mostly in the home or in the office serving tea, and the tolerance for sexual hijinks committed by boyfriends and husbands, even strangers on crowded commuter trains, is much higher among women here than perhaps anywhere else in the world (evidenced by the oft-repeated stories about wives packing condoms into the luggage of husbands embarking on business trips to

Southeast Asia). In much of Asia, especially Japan, sex has never been cast in the dark light it has been in the more puritanical societies of Britain and North America. Christian guilt is missing from Japan's history (at least until it was introduced by the Jesuit missionaries who frowned upon much of Japan's traditional ribaldry from fertility festivals to mixed outdoor bathing).

It must have been a shock for the Christian pioneers to learn of the Shinto story of the creation of Japan, filled with orgies and incest. Buddhism was no better, with its Tachikawa-Ryu sect which embraced sex as an avenue to satori, espousing that Buddhahood resided in a woman's vagina. Then there were such heros as the Zen master Tesshu in the Meiji era who sought enlightenment by attempting to sleep with every courtesan in the country. (He failed, but reported having a great time along the way and discovering that lust is the root of all existence and thus the meaning of Zen.) Perhaps this is why the Jesuits (despite building first-rate universities in Japan) and the more recent battalions of shirt-and-tie Mormon missionaries on bicycles have made little headway in actually converting the Japanese. Homegrown new religions, which don't preach restrictions on sexual behavior, have done much better.

Preachy Westerners, aghast at such Japanese history, should first delve into their own legacies where they will be nonplussed to discover harlots among the holy places of such ancient and sanctified cultures as Rome and Jerusalem. Even in the time of Shakespeare, the convents were places of dubious reputation—ask an English literature scholar, for example, what Hamlet meant when he cried, "Get thee to a nunnery!"

Japan, however, has not escaped immune from the

attempted introduction of supposed Western morals to its shores. The country has always been sensitive to what outsiders think about it, be it mixed public bathing or the consumption of whale meat. Both survive to a limited extent. Since the beginning of the Meiji era (1868–1912), Japan, in its quest to modernize, has sought to embrace Western technology, if not its ideas and moral standards. Unfortunately, with the demise of the shogunate, a romantic chapter of Japanese history which had begun with the melancholic Heian era (794-1185) closed. During the Heian era, polygamy was all the rage among the noble class, a second wife being captured after an exchange of poetic correspondence and a nightly liason or two at the lady's house. For those not in a financial position to afford wives number two, three, and four, ladies of pleasure were abundant and made appearances at parties hosted by the elite.

The Tokugawa era (1600-1868) witnessed the dam bursting on licentiousness. The culture was called *ukiyo*—the floating world and survives today in the erotic prints collectors the world over know as *ukiyo-e*. It was during this time that the geisha came into being. Originally they were male entertainers and a few men actually carried on the tradition until early in the twentieth century. Ironically, Kabuki was orginally performed by women and survived only because men took over all the roles after women were banned from performing. The authorities' decree barring women from the Kabuki stage had nothing to do with poor acting abilities, indeed it was perhaps the opposite. It seems that in the original Kabuki plays, the actresses would mix with the audience after the show giving a more personal and intimate performance of certain scenes they had acted out! The geisha who can perform traditional dances and play the koto or shamisen are now considered virtual anachronisms even by Japanese. Their preferred replacement, young hostesses whose only talent is usually a mediocre *karaoke* rendition of the latest pop hits, seem a poor substitute.

Yet, despite the changes, Japan's love of bawdiness has remained unabated through the turmoil of modernization. On the surface, prostitution was legally eliminated on April Fools Day 1958 with the demise of Tokyo's licensed Yoshiwara brothel district, but the selling of spring, as it has been euphemistically referred to for centuries, continues below the surface and one doesn't have to dig very deep in Tokyo to find a rich river flowing. The Yoshiwara quarter, which had thrived for nearly 350 years, may have disappeared on that spring day in 1958, but its spirit continues to flourish in Shinjuku's Kabukicho district and, to a smaller degree, elsewhere in the metropolis.

Pink Etiquette

This book will give you an outline as to what is available to see and feel, from the mainstream to the offbeat, in Tokyo's thriving world of sex. Tokyo likes to style itself as a faddish city and that usually means that a trend that is here today could likely be gone tomorrow. We will attempt to update this book on a regular basis but it's likely that we won't be able to keep up. (The pace would be exhausting, considering there are tens of thousands of establishments in the metropolitan area "selling spring" or allowing a view of it to one degree or another.) Thus, don't be disappointed if an establishment listed here has closed its doors or been converted into

something else. Who knows, it might even have been changed into something better!

We have catered this book to the foreign traveler and resident whose knowledge of Japanese may be limited.

While *Nihonjin* and the jaded and fluent *gaijin* alike should also find it informative and hopefully educational, it is those with more limited experience and language skills who will likely consider it most valuable. As any long-timer can tell you, being a *gaijin* in Japan can paradoxically be an advantage and a disadvantage. Entering into the sanctum of the *mizushōbai,* the so-called water trade, is no exception. Because you are a foreigner, you may find yourself barred from many establishments. At others, you could end up having the time of your life, being treated like royalty, and having a fellow Japanese customer pick up the tab. You just never know. Yes, you can call it discrimination but Japan regards outsiders as guests—they are to be afforded certain treats and shielded or kept from seeing other things going on behind the paper screens. The optimist gaijin appreciates every new aspect of Japan he is able to discover. The pessimist criticizes his host and mutters about the unfair treatment foreigners receive here. The optimist usually sticks around for a long spell and has a blast. The pessimist usually sooner, rather than later, makes a final trek out to Narita Airport and never returns.

Here are a few tips for the optimists that should afford you better treatment:

• It's almost impossible to overdress for a night on the town even if you are attempting to make your way into the neighborhood peep show. While a tuxedo is never considered de rigeur, the man on the prowl can never go wrong wearing a business suit. Women heading to the host bars should also dress up. You can never go wrong in conservative attire. It will gain you a better chance of entry at the doors of all kinds of establishments.

• A few words of Japanese will usually put touts and mama-sans at ease. The more you know, the more doors will be open to you. There are, in fact, very few establishments in Japan, even in such a supposedly internationalized city as Tokyo, where you are likely to find employees fluent in English. Only a very few of the pink parlors cater especially to foreign tourists, and as is the case almost anywhere in the world, you're likely to do better if you can hang out with the knowing locals.

• Perhaps the best technique in gaining almost unrestricted access in Japan is to have a Japanese escort. A large portion of the most fascinating nightspots are not neccesarily private clubs or "members' only" (despite signs to that effect at the door), but that type of atmosphere certainly prevails. Except for the very casual drinking spots sporting the red lanterns outside and hanging curtains, most nightlife establishments prefer that you be introduced to them by a regular. Japanese are always eager to show a visitor a good time and hauling a foreigner along to their favorite nightspots is a common courtesy. Some of the best finds in this book were discovered in such a fashion.

Fun can still be had in solo excursions. The great thing about being a foreigner in Japan is that you are not expected to know or follow all the rules. As old Japan hands will tell you, sometimes this works in your favor, sometimes it doesn't. Recently, some foreigners have found a chillier reception because of the fear of AIDS.

(Soon Japan will realize that a Japanese is just as likely to be a carrier of the HIV virus as a foreigner.) Also, the influx of so-called guest workers, i.e. illegal aliens, into the country has resulted in an unprecedented posting of rude handwritten "Japanese Only. No Foreigner Allowed" signs at the entrance of many places. It's likely that where you see such a sign, some sap with bad manners has ruined it for the rest of us. Some establishments, both low rent and high class, have a total ban on foreigners, no matter who they are accompanied by, no matter their attire, race, or the size of their bank accounts. You will not get in, period. The optimist knows there's another spot just down the street. The bursting of the bubble economy and a prolonged recession in recent years have forced many previously exclusive establishments to revise downward their prices and to not turn away the well-dressed foreigner. The enlightened proprietors know that money and pleasure speak an international language.

Pink Phrasebook

For a comprehensive list of Japanese pink vocabulary, please consult the glossary. However, here are a few phrases to get you going.

Are foreigners OK?	Gaikoku-jin de mo ii desu ka?
What services do you have?	Donna sābisu ga arimasu ka?
What does ___ mean?	___ 'tte nan desu ka?

How long for ___ yen?	___ en de nan pun gurai narimasu ka?
How much is ___ ?	___ wa ikura desu ka?
Are there any extra charges?	Kore igai ni shiharai ga arimasu ka?
Can I choose my partner?	Aite o erabemasu ka?
I'd like a (young) girl.	(Wakai) ko ga hoshii'n desu ga.
I'd like ___.	___ hoshii'n desu ga.
What are your operating hours?	Eigyō jikan wa itsu desu ka?
Please tell me how to get there.	Michi o oshiete kudasai.
What country are you from?	Dochira no kuni kara desu ka?
I'm American.	Watashi wa Amerika-jin desu.
What's your name?	O-namae wa nan desu ka?
How old are you?	Nan sai desu ka?
Where are you from?	Doko kara kita'n desu ka?

You're beautiful.	Bijin da ne.
You're sexy.	Sekkushi da ne.
I want to have sex with you.	Anata to sekkusu shitai.
I want to sleep with you.	Anata to netai.
I want to hold you.	Daki shimetai.
Can I touch you here?	Koko ni sawatte mo ii?
Can I kiss you?	Kisu shite mo ii?
Can I put it in?	Irete mo ii?
Use a condom	Kondomu o shite.
I want to do it without a condom.	Nama de yaritai.
No way!	Dame!
Use some oil.	Oiru o tsukete.
Don't touch me there!	Asoko ni sawaranaide yo!
Show me your ___.	___ o misete.
Take off your ___.	___ o nuide.
Wonderful, fabulous.	Subarashii, sugoi.

Feels good.	Ii kimochi.
Smells good.	Ii nioi.
Hold me.	Daite.
Give me a hand job.	Shigoite.
Blow me.	Shabutte.
Lick me.	Namete (kure).
Stroke me.	Nadete (kure).
Bite me.	Kande (kure).
Hit me.	Nagutte (kure).
Make me come.	Ikasete.
Wait.	Chotto matte.
Enough!	Mō ii!
Stop!	Yamete!
It hurts!	Itai!
Not yet.	Mada.
Softer.	Motto yasashiku.
Faster.	Motto hayaku.

Slower.	Motto yukkuri.
Deeper.	Motto fukaku.
Stronger.	Motto tsuyoku.
Once more.	Mō ikkai.
Let's do it again.	Mata yarō.
It felt great.	Kimochi yokatta.
It was great.	Tanoshikatta.
It was the best.	Saikō datta.
Till next time.	Mata kondo.

1

HAPPY TALK

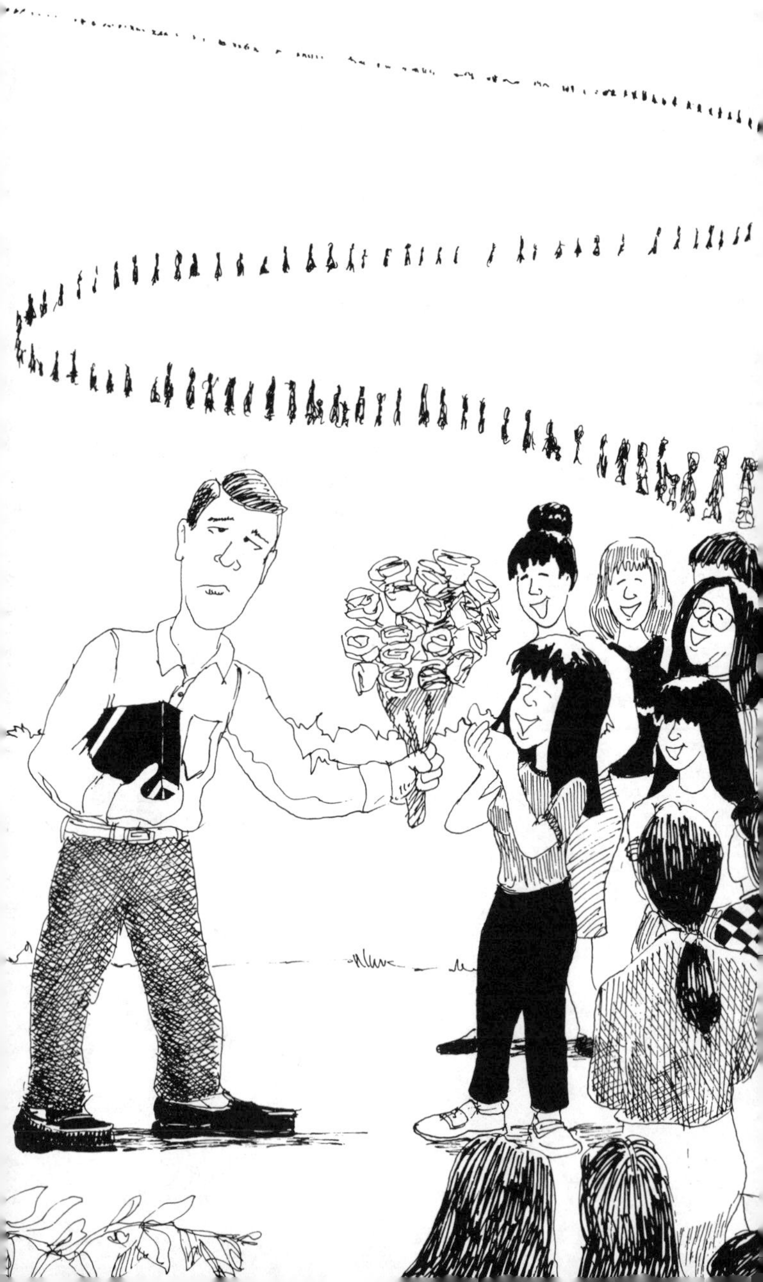

SEX:
THE INTERNATIONAL
LANGUAGE

▼▼▼▼▼▼▼▼▼▼▼▼▼▼▼▼▼▼▼▼▼▼▼▼▼▼▼▼▼

Part of the fantasy of the adolescent male in becoming a famous rock star or an all-star lineman are the fringe benefits, namely, the groupies. Unfortunately, few of us have the talent or the perseverance to make it to the big leagues. Reality dawns upon us as we finish school. We realize our destiny will have nothing to do with fancy guitar chords or scoring the goal that wins the World Cup. We suddenly wake up one morning realizing that we are accountants or software engineers, toiling in obscurity. Never will we enjoy, as Kiss did, the legion of pubescent plaster casters. Never will we find outside the locker room a league of women following us around from city to city who know our award-winning statistics and are eager to show us theirs. We are left to pursue the women who want us for just what we are or what we have.

A lot of us don't have that much to offer to the women who prefer material things—no fancy sports cars, no plush lodge in the mountains, no platinum cards. It sometimes can be slim pickings. Some of us, because of professional opportunity or desperation, trudge off to Japan and find ourselves in what we initially perceive to be one of the least glamorous jobs in the world—English teaching. The uninitiated are stunned. They stand before a class of beautiful but mute young women. The tutorial seems to last for an eternity. After a few months, the newly arrived Brit or American has become desperate. There seems to be not an iota of progress.

As usual, one day after class, Kimiko, a petite twenty-year-old who works part time in a flower shop, is at the *sensei's* desk asking, it seems, the same question for the twentieth time about conjugating a particular verb. Today she seems particularly flustered. "Jeemu-*sensei,* I need extra help I sink," she says. Did she just ever so slightly brush her breasts up against my side, Jim says to himself. He thinks, maybe it is just his vivid imagination conspiring with his raging hormones. After all, he hasn't gotten laid since he's been here. How do you ask out these beautiful nubile girls, he wonders. "Well Kimiko I think it's a left brain, right brain problem. You know English apparently must be learned from the other side of your brain." Jim has seen this in various books he is reading in a desperate attempt to find out why his class can't learn. Jim is about to conclude perhaps he is just a failure as a language teacher, something that might be connected to the fact that the only related training he ever had for this job was a freshman college class in public speaking. "Jeemu you are a bery good teacher. I sink if we spend more time together I will make fast progress more." She *is* rubbing up against him! He tries to correct her grammar. "You will progress more fast, uh, I mean, you faster more progress, yes." Kimiko is looking up at him and smiling. Jim may be a little rattled but he's no idiot. He knows he is being flashed an international signal. "Kimiko, would you like to have coffee or something at a *kissaten?* I mean, uh, to discuss this further?" Kimiko nods her head ever so slightly and their eyes make contact for a brief instant. Jim will soon realize he will never have a problem getting laid in Japan again. He will quickly discover that he has one of the world's greatest jobs—he is getting paid to pick up girls.

Tony Watson (not his real name) has been teaching English in Tokyo since before most of his current students were born. Although he speaks quite fluent Japanese, he has never lost his Tennessee drawl in English and his taste for Jack Daniels whiskey. One night, mixing the whiskey and water in one of his favorite Shibuya hangouts, we talk about his experiences. Tony is currently living with a mid-twenties Japanese lady who is one of the most beautiful and sexy women I have ever seen. He's left her at home tonight to speak frankly. "I'd have to be an idiot to go back to the States," the balding, sandy-haired American says, clinking another ice cube into his glass. "I realized that in my prime I never would have been able to get, let alone find, the types of girls that are here." And things have gotten better, not worse, as Tony has gotten older. "Well, first of all, the girls are more beautiful than they used to be. They have better legs. Because of the diet and all, nowadays you don't see as many *daikon ashi* (stumpy fat legs) girls. Take a stroll through Roppongi, half the girls are *bodicon*, wearing scanty body-hugging outfits and they look terrific. I'm not a young man anymore but I've got the routine down. I could probably pick up a girl in ten minutes in Roppongi if I wanted to." In a nutshell, Tony discovered a long time ago that just being an

English teacher qualifies him to have groupies. "Yeh, what a great way to go through life," he says laughing in between puffs on a Marlboro. "No, I'll never go back. I'm going to die a happy man here."

For the novice or the veteran, a casual affair or a permanent girlfriend is usually sitting out there in the classroom even if she seems to be wearing a mask of disinterest through the 50-minute sessions. Not everyone can or wants to teach English (or French, Italian, or Swahili) in Japan. That, however, doesn't preclude the rest of the *gaijin* crowd from reaping the benefits. Tokyo is dotted with English conversation lounges. Typically, they charge a reduced flat-fee for admission to foreigners (usually ¥350-¥700) which might include unlimited coffee or tea, and a pricier by-the-hour entrance charge for Japanese. The foreigners are expected to do nothing more than speak in their native language to the native visitors. Some of the female Japanese patrons are merely looking to brush up their language skills or to attempt to converse with a living, breathing foreigner. They sometimes visit from neighboring prefectures—Chiba, Saitama, and Kanagawa—where opportunities to meet native English speakers are rarer than in Tokyo. Others are *gaijin* groupies who desire nothing more than to enjoy sexual congress with exotic (i.e. non-Asian) men. Some even have particular predilections, tall fellows, black men, or those with lots of body hair (although most Japanese women seem to prefer those whose chests are follicularly challenged). While it is unusual but not impossible to troll a lovely out of the lounge and into a love hotel the same evening, the standard operating procedure is to exchange phone numbers and/or make a date for some other night. Within a couple of meetings it will certainly be clear whether the lass is interested only in your conversational abilities or those of a more intimate nature.

For those who just can't bear to enter a place where essentially they have to masquerade as English teacher on the meter, there are a number of other establishments in Tokyo which have gained a reputation as prime spots where young Japanese women on the prowl go to meet foreign men. At one time, certain discos in Akasaka and Roppongi met this criterion; it is less the case these days. Many women actually go to discos to do nothing more than dance with each other. Men find it hard to get a dance or a word in edgewise. Other establishments, such as Charleston or Deja Vu in Roppongi, Aspen Glow in Shibuya, or the gay-turned-reggae club 69 in Shinjuku, despite being listed in other guide books as popular hunting grounds, are well past their prime. I hesitate to select only a few to include in the contemporary hit list. It's like a fad portrayed on the cover of *Time* magazine—by the time it hits print it is already passé. Another fear is that publicizing something that has been merely word of mouth will ruin it. On the condition that every horny male reading this book agrees not to converge on these establishments on the same night— I will name names. Agreed? Sure, right.

The current number one is no big secret since every visitor and local ends up there eventually just to say they've been there. But it also seems to attract an inordinate number of beautiful (although a bit slutty, according to many critics) free-spirited young Japanese women. It is the Hard Rock Cafe. If you don't mind competing with US Marines (just don't get drunk and call them "bloody jarheads") and watching the girl you are pursuing bounce off other men around the crowded bar like a hockey puck, the Tokyo branch of the chain world famous for its T-shirts is the place for you. I have personally witnessed a colleague of mine on several occasions end up leaving with a woman after less than ten minutes at the bar! "I can usually tell within a few minutes if they're game but I hang around for another few minutes just to make it not look so obvious to the girl," he says. Yeh, sure.

The present number two is an eclectic establishment close to Ogikubo Station called the Library. It is the personal domain of proprietor David G. (for God) Munoz, a literate but tough-as-nails Vietnam veteran, who makes no secret that he has first crack at any hot-looking babe that walks in the bar. On some nights there's a lot to go around so this isn't a problem. If he likes you, David will even point out the young ladies he knows are amenable and perhaps put in a good word for you in Japanese. On other nights the atmosphere can be a bit ugly with rugby-type smashed Irishmen with no visible means of support glaring down at intoxicated North American computer programmers. Munoz has no qualms (nor lack of brawn) about stepping in and breaking up the ensuing fights. A word of warning: anyone not up to Munoz's standards of behavior (which can vary widely from night to night) may find themselves summarily ejected. After all, as big Dave proclaims, the Library is now a members' club. The best advice for first-timers (who need not show a membership card): cuddle up in the corner with one of the hundreds of used paperbacks for sale and take some time to figure out the place. It is a very unique Tokyo hangout.

MEET MARKET

▼▼▼▼▼▼▼▼▼▼▼▼▼▼▼▼▼▼▼▼▼▼▼▼▼▼▼▼▼▼

It seemed the answer to every bashful man's dream—a simple way to meet a pretty girl with minimal risk of rejection. The admission was under ¥1000 and the cashier explained that after the first 45 minutes an extra ¥1500 would be added on for each hour I remained. Simple enough it seemed and a hell of a lot cheaper than the run of the mill Tokyo hostess bar. But in the back of my mind, I figured, there had to be a catch.

I was seated on a long sofa extending down one side of the room. There were five tables on my side at each of which sat a guy. In the middle of each table a large sign jutted out with a number on it that was clearly visible on the other side of the room (about five meters away) where young ladies sat behind tables. The women, who appeared to be mostly in the late teens and early twenties, sat behind tables which also displayed big signs with a number. I immediately focused on Miss Five. I knew that the women were not employees of the establishment but were also customers who were charged a much smaller flat fee.

The game works like this. When a guy spots a lady he is interested in talking with he fills out a small pink form on his table and hands it to the *maître d'*-looking fellow who is in charge of the whole affair. To fill out the form requires a rudimentary knowledge of reading kanji. You are asked to write in the number of the lady you desire to meet, list your zodiac birth year (example rooster or rat), blood type, and your hobbies. By the time I had figured out what I was supposed to write after slowly reading my way through the form I noticed that a gentleman from my side of the establishment was cozying up next to lovely Miss Five! It was here that it sunk in that being a faster reader of kanji can have its advantages. Although my heart sunk, it wasn't a few seconds later before I realized that after my second straight shot of bourbon, little Miss Nine wasn't looking too bad either. My heart began racing as I wrote her number on my pink pad. I put myself down as an alumnus of the Year of the Boar and mentioned reading as my hobbies. But I was at a total loss for the blood-type answer. Honestly, to this day, I have no idea what my blood type is although I know that it's not one of those rare ones like ABO (if there is such a thing). I do know that Japanese consider this information vital for assessing a person's personality but can't recall whether an A-blooded man is the hot blooded and off the handle type or is romantic, quiet, and a true gentleman. I did what any honest bloke would do and placed a question mark next to the blood type. The *maître d'* took my form over to Miss Nine, and without even glancing over at me she quickly filled out a reply. Mr. D' brought it back to me without a trace of emotion on his face (although I'm certain he snuck a peak at her answer). She had circled

Name _____
Zodiac Sign _____
Age _____ Rh _____
Blood Type _____ Temp ___K°
Cholesterol Count (Metric) _____
Height in Kilometers _____ Weight in Yen _____
What is Your Sixth Favorite Color? _____
Why? _____
Favorite Diet Member _____
His Bank Account Number _____
Why are you wasting your time here? _____→
PLEASE SEE REVERSE SIDE FOR MORE POINTLESS QUESTIONS

the "I'm sorry" reply. My heart sank again. Actually I was more embarrassed than heartbroken to have been rejected in such a fashion. But could I really blame Miss Nine? After all I was not only a foreigner of dubious repute but a human being who did not have a clue as to his blood type. This dilemma forced me to resort to what all men must do in such dire situations—I lied.

After another shot of the brown liquid, a new entrant was seated in front of the number two placard. Although by no means a raving beauty, I instantly decided to select her. After all someone else might soon choose her and I could not leave the joint totally humiliated. For Miss Two's perusal I informed her on my pink sheet that I was born in the Year of the Cock, was a Type-A blood carrier and my hobby was traveling to expensive international resorts. It worked. For the privilege of chatting up fresh Miss Two, I was required to buy her a ladies drink and a ladies snack. Ah, I was beginning to see how these places made their money. The combination of one round of food and drink quickly set me back ¥2500 and not to mention that I was now running up a time tab since my initial 45 minutes had expired. Miss Two, whose real name was Sachiko (or so she said) was 19 and living with her parents in Saitama Prefecture. It took me another hour to realize that she ventured into these types of establishment not to meet men but to seek refuge from the streets until the first train back to the countryside left Shinjuku Station. What better way to while away the time than by having strange men buy you food and drink all night long? Of course, none stuck around for very long realizing that as the meter was ticking they had no chance of getting the sweet young Miss to accompany them to a nearby love hotel. Perhaps some guys do succeed in convincing the ladies of the meet club to head out with them, but in the couple of hours I spent there I did not see it happen.

HOSTESS BARS

▼▼▼▼▼▼▼▼▼▼▼▼▼▼▼▼▼▼▼▼▼▼▼▼▼▼▼▼▼▼

Perhaps the most baffling aspect of the Tokyo pink world to the foreign greenhorn is why Japanese men go to hostess bars. After all, for about the same amount of money (even less in some cases) you can get laid or get a wonderful allover massage from a naked woman who will end the experience with at least a hand job. Another alternative for less money is the strip shows and nude theatres. So why would a fellow hand over money just to have some young woman in a cocktail dress spend the evening massaging little more than his ego?

For a long time this was an unanswered question for me too. Now after months of spending many nights in almost every kind of *mizushōbai* institution imaginable and meeting hundreds of men and women who frequent such establishments as patrons and employees, I think I know the answer—hostess bars are relaxing environments in a way that no soapland or nude show can match. The skeptics out there are probably thinking I've been in Tokyo too long and have turned into a paler reflection of the typical salaryman. Not so, I protest. I must confess, however, that I have come to enjoy the traditional hostess bars more and more—especially the kind where I know that there is no pressure on me or the "hostitute" girl to talk each other into a short-time date, meaning a ¥30,000 tryst at the love hotel around the corner. I can drink what I like, as long as I like, make small talk with a variety of women, banter with the inebriated salaryman across the room, and sing a few off-key *karaoke* songs in the language of my choice (many places nowadays feature tunes not only in Japanese and English but also in Korean, Cantonese, Thai, and Tagalog—Tagalog being my second personal favorite because all the songs seem to be in my flat key and the words are even easier to pronounce than Spanish).

Even though I've caught the hostess bar bug, I am not dying of it. I avoid the exorbitantly priced Ginza and Akasaka clubs unless I am being treated by my very wealthy Japanese friend, Mr. Y. (I still don't know exactly what he does for a living and I'm not sure I should ask. But I am curious as to where he got the money after the bubble burst to build a five-story house in Tokyo bigger than anything I've ever seen in Beverly Hills.) For those who will never get the chance to visit a ¥100,000 per visit Ginza or Akasaka hostess bar, I can assure you that it is decidedly not worth the ticket of admission unless you are on expense account or someone else is footing the bill. Sure, the young ladies are a little classier, mama-san has a very nice kimono, and there may even be a tuxedo-clad *gaijin* tinkling at the Steinway as you sip your Remy Martin XO cognac, but it is not that much more upscale than the places in Ikebukero where the tab is likely to only be a tenth of that of such ritzy joints.

However, the foreign fellow in Tokyo who is interested in doing the hostess bar gig or is looking for a spot to economically entertain visiting bosses or clients whose command of Japanese is nil, and would have their puritanical senses overloaded by some of the other spots detailed in this book, will be grateful to know that I have just the place for you—the Filipina hostess bars. As Japan's yen rises in value and the economy struggles to decide whether it has bottomed out, a number of hostess clubs have thrown their native talent out on the streets and replaced them with a lineup of more affordable recruits from the friendly isles of the Philippines. Unlike the predominantly Thai clubs, Filipinas in Tokyo in the nineties usually don't work in clubs that are merely fronts for prostitution but instead are friendly young ladies who are truly fond of nice men. Now some of the young ladies from the Philippines may have done their stints as "exotic dancers" in the raunchy prostitution fronts of Manila's Ermita district but many are college educated, even virgins, who have come to Japan out of economic necessity. The lucky ones find themselves working in Tokyo clubs where they hostess and nothing more. Many a *gaijin* fellow has found a nice girlfriend in such establishments, slowly falling in love while whiling away the evenings with a seductive young lady who speaks fluent English, can sing *karaoke* in several languages, and knows how to flirt while maintaining the demureness of her strict Catholic upbringing. A customer who makes himself a regular in the Filipina hostess bars can ask for a regular to sit with him (usually there's an extra ¥2000 charge for such a request) and the young woman will be flattered by the exclusive attention and the object of envy of her colleagues. The

Filipina looks upon the North American and European male as a prize catch and to marry such a guy would literally be a dream come true for her. More and more are ending up getting hitched to Japanese men as economic ties and personal relationships tighten between Tokyo and Manila. But even the lowly *gaijin* English teacher has perhaps as much status in the beautiful eyes of the Filipina as a Japanese company president. Yes, there still is justice in this world.

A few pointers are in order for any lad who'd like to strike a more than fleeting romance with a Filipina working in Tokyo. The first thing to remember is that although the young lady may come from a relatively poor third world country she comes from a culture rich in etiquette and protocol. Unless the woman is anything other than a so-called "hostitute" you will not get anywhere on the first night. Do not be tempted to ask her home after you have just met her. She may act like she is flattered by the request but something inside of her will recoil and she may regard you from now on as nothing more than an unsophisticated rake. If you are very lucky and make a flattering impression she will ask for your phone number or may give you her name card and covertly write her home number on it. If that doesn't happen the first time you stop by, ask for hers or volunteer your number the second night you venture into her hostess bar. Again it is important to recall that Philippine culture has emerged out of a mixture of Spanish, American, Chinese, and Malay influences with perhaps the first two predominating in the social arena—nineteenth-century Spain and 1950s America. After the second or third meeting it is proper for you to ask her out for a date on her day off—usually Sunday. A "no" reply would definitely mean "no" but don't take a "yes" as a definite green light.

You should plan to take her to an impressive eatery as this is the point where you really can begin to woo the young lady, but true Philippine courtship, be reminded, is in a bit of a time warp. Don't be surprised if she shows up with a couple of female co-workers or an aunt living in Saitama. If she shows up at all consider yourself lucky. But if she is a no-show do not consider yourself out of luck. I found this out the hard way one time during a trip to Hong Kong, where many Filipinas work as domestics. I had made the acquaintance of a beautiful young woman at a Wanchai nightclub frequented by single Filipina maids. I was so wowed by her that I asked her to meet me the following evening for dinner at my five-star hotel on the Kowloon side. I told her I would come back early from a business appointment in Macau especially to meet her at a reasonable hour. She agreed. However she never showed. The following evening back at the same club I ran into some of her friends and explained what happened. They then explained the standards of Philippine courting behavior to me. No, I should not have expected her to appear because I would not even be taken seriously until I had made repeated invitations to her. It was assumed by her and all her friends that my initial invitation was likely nothing more than what is called in Tagalog, *bula bula* (what the Japanese call *gomasuri*, roughly equivalent to good ol' American bullshitting). Thus, if I really wanted to go out with the young lady, I would have to make another attempt to set up a date and perhaps another. Unfortunately I had to leave Hong Kong before I could carry through on the ritual.

Back in Tokyo the game is played in perhaps a bit more abbreviated fashion. Filipinas living here have learned that Japanese rules are expected to be followed, meaning that one is to keep one's word and show up on the appointed day, if not the precise scheduled time. Many Western men are willing to jump through the hoops held up by the coy but wily Filipinas. These are the type of men who have grown weary of Japanese women, considering them too introverted and lacking in passion. On the other hand there is a scarcity of Western women and many are happy to be away from the ladies of their home countries whom they are apt to label as schizophrenic, neurotic, or overly brash.

The Filipinas are regarded as something in between the two extremes—affectionate and spicy. There are indeed different strokes for different folks and there are those men who spend their entire assignments in Japan never expressing interest in Japanese or other Asian women. They are rare, but they do exist. I know of one American fellow who over a two-year period managed to have a string of relationships in Tokyo with a Ghanian, an Italian, and an Israeli before finally seeming to settle down with a Canadian. Yes, Tokyo has indeed become a bit internationalized and at first read it would seem safe to assume that my friend didn't move here from New York City for the women. The funny thing is he met all the aforementioned ladies at a hostess bar in Ikebukuro, appropriately named Club Universal.

THE TROPIC OF CANCER

▼▼▼▼▼▼▼▼▼▼▼▼▼▼▼▼▼▼▼▼▼▼▼▼▼▼▼▼▼▼

Hostess bars in Tokyo should be shunned by the foreign visitor unless he is dragged along by a Japanese colleague who is footing the bill. After all, they are hideously expensive (upwards of ¥100,000 per visit per person) and while light physical contact is tolerated, in some classy establishments it can be frowned upon. A few of Tokyo's hostess bars have real character, less outrageous prices and beautiful women who wouldn't mind a date with a dashing *gaijin*. (The tip-off, usually, is when asked if you would be so kind as to give them an English lesson, the protocol is to always say yes, that you'd be happy to conjugate verbs with them, even if you happen to be a mid-level executive with an American computer company.) Even fewer hostess bars are a must-visit, or an experience that you will remember for a lifetime and emerge from a more educated man of the world. The only such haunt measuring up to this billing I have found in Japan is the Tropic of Cancer in Roppongi, next to the Hard Rock Cafe. The reference to the great erotic author Henry Miller, in this case, is not a rip-off and is especially endearing once you get to know the story. At the piano sits a woman who will be remembered not for her music but as a footnote to literary and perhaps art history. There are those listening to Hoki Tokuda who believe that she gave her late husband Henry Miller an appropriate swan song. Others feel that Henry's last wife should occupy a place in history along with Circe and Salome. Only one conclusion seems certain—she imposed a sexual frustration on the famous novelist of epic proportions.

Henry, at the age of 74 in 1965, began personally documenting his unrequited passion in near daily letters to the 28-year-old Japanese singer soon after her arrival in Hollywood. "It was like a tragedy if I think about it now, because I didn't understand him. I just tried to escape from him," she says while holding court in her nightclub. There is a look of regret on her face as she recalls how she tried to give the famed author, nearly 45 years her senior, the brushoff. But in typical Japanese fashion, Hoki tried to be polite and just couldn't bring herself to tell Henry to forget her. Henry idealized her as some kind of innocent geisha princess. His writings show he had long been fascinated with Japan but he never came here because of repeated warning from astrologer Sydney Omar that such a trip would end in tragedy, according to Tokuda.

These days Hoki is glad Henry never accepted the numerous offers he had to tour Japan because the fan of Lady Murasaki's romantic Heian era would have been sorely disappointed by the materialistic drab Japan of the mid-twentieth century. Tokuda says she was anything but a typical Japanese young woman in Miller's presence. "I gave him a real bad time. He became an insomniac," Tokuda recalls. "He couldn't sleep so he painted about Japan because he saw me as a typical Japanese girl, but as you can see I am not," she says with a laugh. Tokuda, now 55, remains boisterous, perhaps a very apropos personality for a mama-san who presides over a glitzy bar filled with foreign hostesses favored by Tokyo's writers, musicians, and even a mob boss or two.

During the two-year courtship, she agreed to see Henry once or twice a week but the sex-crazed author didn't get to touch her, a cause of tremendous frustration expressed in the frequent letters he sent her. After the courtship she agreed to marry him but she set down strict platonic conditions for the relationship. "We had separate bedrooms and I brought a girlfriend with me to live in his house." She laughs again. "But he seemed happy, maybe because all of a sudden he had two young Japanese girls in his house." While it was hands off with his wife, he'd occasionally paw an agreeable Puko, the roommate, according to Tokuda. She confirms that by that time the author of so many sexually explicit novels was impotent. "That's right. But he was talking about it all the time, morning and night. He always very openly talked about sex."

The platonic ménage à trois stayed intact for three years but the sexless marriage and subsequent close friendship between Henry and Hoki ran for a total of eleven years. During the marriage Henry found another outlet for his pent-up energy. He became a prolific painter, sometimes completing five watercolors a day. Tokuda, as she glances at the art works on the wall of her bar, remembers that Miller seemed happy only when he painted. "He'd sing, sometimes even dance. He'd make noises or scream 'heh, heh, heh,'" she recalls. "I guess it gave him a sort of pleasure, more pleasure than writing. Writing was work." In one published comment about painting, Miller said, "To paint is to love again. It's only when we look with eyes of love that we see as the painter sees."

The walls of the Tropic of Cancer are covered with some of Henry's watercolors and lithographs. Others are for sale down the road at Tokuda's Big Sur Henry Miller Memorial Gallery in the Azabu Juban district. A visit there is a requisite for anyone exploring the erotica of this city. Miller started painting in his thirties and by the time he died at the age of 88 in 1980 he had completed several thousand pictures. He counted many artists among his friends during his Paris days and was clearly influenced or received advice from the likes of John Dudley, Abraham Rattner, and Hiler Hilaire.

Most of the hostesses (hands off, please) in the Tropic of Cancer weren't even born when their boss met Miller. A few profess ignorance of who he was and know nothing of the amazing story of Miller and their employer. One young brunette, from the American Midwest, is apparently the only of Hoki's employees who has read any of Miller's books. She isn't impressed. "It's typical male stuff, I find it disgusting," she says sipping a glass of red wine. "The graphic sex aside, what about the wordplay and his wonderfully anarchic philosophy of life?" I ask, fishing for some redemption of one of my literary heroes. "A lot of it is rambling drivel. The rest he stole from Dostoyevski and Knut Hamsun." Ouch. She agrees, however, that Henry's watercolors are actually pretty good. Glancing at them on the walls we compare Miller to Picasso, Miro, and the Dadaists.

Perusing the Tokyo gallery and a catalogue of most

of his surviving pieces it appears that the majority of them, at least those painted until the late 1960s, are surprisingly nonerotic. Portraits of fully clothed women, villages, and fish are recurring subjects. But those (mainly with Japanese titles) from after the time he became obsessed with Hoki are more graphic. *Asamara* (Japanese for morning erection), done in 1969, features Miller's signature around an erect penis in the upper left side of the painting. Even more explicit is *Kirai Desuka* (Do you hate me?) dedicated to Hoki in 1971 which Miller wrote was a profile of his fantasy. It includes a semi-erect male organ, two naked women with attention drawn to their genitals, as well as a disembodied red vagina.

Tokuda is trying to reacquire the paintings Miller gave away over the years as payment to milkmen, taxi drivers, and bartenders. The typical lithograph in the Tokyo gallery sells, on average, for ¥70,000. Collectors quickly snap up the few originals which surface from dens or are discovered in attics in France and California, paying upwards of $10,000 for them. Tokuda says she plans to retire in a few years to California where she has maintained a permanent residence since the mid-sixties. "I want to open a Henry Miller gallery there, too, perhaps in Carmel," she says as she returns to the piano.

Asked to play something that reminds her of her famed late husband, she begins singing "My Heart Belongs to Daddy." For Henry Miller this public display of affection comes more than a decade too late.

2

THE EYES HAVE IT

PEEP SHOWS

▼▼▼▼▼▼▼▼▼▼▼▼▼▼▼▼▼▼▼▼▼▼▼▼▼▼▼▼▼▼

In a recent magazine advertisement for a brand name
VHS camera, a beautiful young woman clad in blue
jeans and a maroon sweater is caught in the process of
taking off the upper garment. In the single frame, her
eyes are fixed on the unseen photographer, her lips are
passive, sporting neither a smile nor a frown. The ad, in
Japanese, touts the new and improved high quality
"distinct color viewfinder." But the biggest letters are
reserved for the banner phrase which can be best trans-
lated as "If you peep, you'll understand."

The $1,800 VHS camera, according to the rest of the
copy which makes numerous references to the
instrument's refined "peeping" ability, clearly seems to
have been designed for the kind of fellow who enjoys
standing underneath a woman's window and finds pleasure in catching a glimpse of her undressing. Now,
thanks to Mitsubishi's Miracleshot, he can watch the
scene over and over in the privacy of his own room! For
Japanese who view the ad, it is no shock and they are
truly amazed to hear from Americans and Europeans

that this type of commercial presentation would be virtually taboo in other countries and generate immense criticism from people in many walks of life. In Japan, however, the Mitsubishi Miracleshot advertisement merges a hi-tech innovation with an old native tradition.

Voyeurism has a noble history in Japan. A custom originiating in villages many hundreds of years ago, called *yobai* (night creeping), has only disappeared in recent decades. On a *yobai* mission the fellows of the town would head to the houses of the single women and, one by one, stealthily make their way into their homes. The custom was for the ladies not to refuse them and many a young woman, in search of just the right long-time companion, would treat herself to several samplings a night. A fellow waiting his turn, just outside the home or perhaps in another room, could be expected to monitor by sight and sound the goings-on initiated by his predecessor.

Among the nobles of the upper classes it was also not uncommon to have an unparticipating party in the room while sex was going on. Royalty and shoguns frequently had a maid, out of sight behind a small partition, tracking their couplings. It was important to record these love-making sessions with courtesans incase an offspring resulted. Apparently the well-to-do in Japan back then were not immune from a prototype of the paternity suit.

The tradition of peeping continues to this day as many foreign women residing in Japan are aghast to find out and then suffer the double indignity of finding police not equally outraged when they attempt to file a report about the neighborhood peeping Tom.

Fortunately there is a healthier outlet for the fellow who likes to watch women undress—*nozoki*—(peep shows) abound in Tokyo, especially in the Shinjuku and Ikebukero districts. They are also among the city's best bargains on excursions to paint the town pink. The modern-day peeper is lured into the *nozoki* establishment by a barker or a broadcast from an excitied voice on a tape loop espousing the thrill that awaits him inside. Up the elevator he goes and pays the cashier. Sometimes the entrance fee is as low as ¥2,000. He then takes a seat on a long sofa with several other chaps waiting for the current performance to end. The customers can while away the time reading one of the weekly soft-porn magazines or viewing the pink movie being screened on the television set in the waiting lounge.

Finally it's time. The fellows are escorted into their personal booths, containing a small stool, a tissue box on the window ledge, and trash can which is nearly overflowing with used tissues. The booth appears to have one-way glass since it's impossible to see into the other booths on the other side of the small stage. At the center of the stage a towel lies on the ground and off to the side are a couple of small stuffed animals.

A young woman emerges, she appears to be not much older than a teenager but she's not that attractive. She begins to disrobe, quickly revealing that her best attributes are beneath her bra. Ample cup sizes are rare in Japan and men are willing to overlook other less than adequate body parts if a young woman has big breasts, known in Japanese-English as "milkcans." Miss Milkcans is dancing her way around the room going through an amateurish performance of slowly but clumsily removing her bra and see-through panties. Suddenly there's a knock on the door. The veteran is not surprised. He knows that the door is about to be opened by a beautiful woman. Perhaps today she'll be wearing that flimsy red number. She is and asks, as usual, "do you want the service?" It's little more than the admission price and it's the reason most men are repeat customers to the peep shows. As soon as she is handed the money she says she'll be right back and like a nurse preparing for the busy doctor's entrance, instructs the patient to pull down his pants in the meantime.

Back on stage, the young woman is down to her panties and massaging herself as she continues the circuit. She stops briefly in front of each window, staring vacantly upwards. There's again a knock at the door and the beautiful woman in the red dress enters. As requested, the customer has already drawn his trousers and underpants to his knees. The woman in red plunks down on the ledge several plastic-sealed wet-wipes and a bottle which appeared to orginally have contained honey. She quickly rips three tissues from the box on the ledge and expertly goes to work after squirting an oily liquid from the bottle onto her hands. Permission to touch her is granted although she warns that "only on top" is permitted. Customers who zip down her top and reach in to touch her breast receive a frown—apparently on top refers to no touching of skin. The ban is widely flaunted and there's no enforced penalty. Even the most jaded client is amazed to discover that in what seems like less than 45 seconds she has completed the job to full satisfaction. She is to be commended as a skilled professional. She appreciates the compliment as she tidies up and flicks the wet wipes and tissues into the trash can. She bids adieu to the satisfied customer who notices the show on stage is ending with Miss Milkcans collapsing on the towel after bringing herself to a "climax." The lights go on. Precisely ten minutes have elapsed since the men entered the booths.

STRIP SHOWS

▼▼▼▼▼▼▼▼▼▼▼▼▼▼▼▼▼▼▼▼▼▼▼▼▼▼▼▼

F ads come and go in the pink world but one mainstay
for not only decades, but centuries, has been the strip
show. The Meiji era had its *miseimono* stages at festivals
where ladies would hike up their kimonos for the
appreciative crowd. The Heisei era carries on the tradition with the ladies likely to be dressing (or perhaps it's
better to say undressing) in the latest Western fashions.
Taking its cue from New York where the El Morocco,
once the city's exclusive nightclub of the rich and
famous, has become an upscale strip bar, many Tokyo
nightspots are trying to add a classier image to their strip
shows by importing foreign dancers and expensive light
shows.

However, with the bursting of the bubble economy,
these high-priced Las Vegas style attractions probably
won't last long. The mainstays are the back alley *nūdo
gekijo* which should be a must-visit for every foreign
male. However, it is not usually the dancers who provide the most eye-popping entertainment for the *gaijin*
novitiate but the behavior of the audience. The danc-

ers—most of whom really can't dance very well—usually emerge on the stage to the pounding of a Donna Summer or Madonna record and go through a few perfunctory moves with their feet before shedding their garments. Unlike at a Western striptease act where the men hoot and holler to encourage the dancer on and communicate their sexual fantasies with their eyes to the unclad beauty on stage, the men in Japan watch virtually without emotion, voices silent, eyes fixed on the woman. There is sometimes polite applause when the panties are finally removed but much of the time the audience reacts with silence and a slight shifting of the eyes to her freshly revealed pubic region.

At most strip joints these days select members of the audience are treated to a special close-up look of gynecological dimensions. Mariko will plop herself down in front of an audience member, hand him a magnifying glass and allow him to get a voyeuristic eyeful for about 10 to 15 seconds before taking back the instrument and moving down the row to the next lucky fellow. Other clubs have the girls handing their customers a Polaroid camera and inviting them to snap close-up pictures of their vaginas. One can only wonder what these guys end up doing with their photographic souvenirs.

Although almost all of the nudie spots tolerate well-behaved (that means no animalistic hooting or loud laughing) foreign men there is one joint in Shinjuku's Kabukicho which actively encourages *gaijin* patrons. DX Kabukicho even places discount coupons in some Tokyo English-language tourist periodicals offering ¥1000 off the normal admission price of ¥5000. Who said there are no breaks for foreigners in Japan's pink world?

Outside of Tokyo is where it really gets raunchy. Chiba, Kanagawa, and Saitama prefectures abound with shows where audience members are hauled on stage to engage in sex with the ladies. Before pulling out your JR map to find the express routes to Kawasaki or East Chiba City be aware that such public acts are illegal and the shows are occasionally busted by the police. The sometimes well-publicized dragnets have ended up snaring famous and not-so-famous TV talents, respected professors, and even police officers. Although being busted for banging a stripper on stage (if this happens to be your peccadillo) will provide for some interesting press clippings to send to select friends back home, it probably won't help your case when you next visit Immigration to extend your visa.

3

▼▼▼▼▼▼▼▼▼▼▼▼▼▼▼▼▼▼▼▼▼▼▼▼▼▼▼▼▼▼

GETTING A FEEL FOR IT

CABARET

▼▼▼▼▼▼▼▼▼▼▼▼▼▼▼▼▼▼▼▼▼▼▼▼▼▼▼▼▼▼▼

I am permitted to enter the London Cabaret in Tokyo's Shibuya district only after assuring the manager at the door that I can speak Japanese. He's upfront about the prices, always a good sign of a reputable establishment. It's ¥4000 for conversation and all I can drink in the next hour but if I want the *enchō* (extended service) it's another ¥12,000. I pay the ¥4000 upfront and am led to a seat. I know that if I desire, at the very least, I will be entitled to a hand job for the *enchō*

As I pass through the reception area, two relatively rotund and unattractive women on the sofa stand up and give me the enthusiastic *"irasshaimase"* welcome. I mutter to myself that I hope I won't have to be entertained by either of them. I am in luck, as a beautiful, very thin woman soon sits down in the booth seat next to me. I glance at her and then at the wall and notice a poster of a topless woman.

"I'm Sayori, nice to meet you," she says. I introduce myself and notice that Sayori is very, very thin—too thin as a matter of fact. Her legs could make her this year's poster child for anorexia. In the dim light it's hard to guess her age by looking at her face. By taking in her mannerisms and voice I surmise that she's about 30. Sayori and I hit it off well. She seems to really enjoy talking with a rare foreigner in her cabaret. She's serving me endless beers and asking the routine questions that Japanese always ply *gaijin* with—what kinds of Japanese foods I like, how long I've been here, and what do I think of the country. Sometimes such questions, proffered over and over again, can be annoying but with Sayori I've got no hesitation about answering. After all, it opens the gate for me to ask her some probing questions.

In the next booth an inebriated fellow in his fifties is pawing at one of the zaftig girls. It's not long before she has got the top of her dress around her waist and from the motion of her right hand I can tell she's trying to get the guy to a climax as quickly as possible.

Sayori is originally from Fukushima Prefecture, an area known as Tohoku, a sort of Japanese Appalachia. She's delighted to hear that I was in her hometown of Koriyama only a couple of months ago. We talk about a myriad of things as she seems quite the conversationalist. She's very curious about the American education system and one branch of the conversation leads to another and it isn't long before I've learned that Sayori lost her virginity at 19 (she remains bashful about giving her current age) and makes about ¥500,000 a month serving up beer, conversation, and hand jobs.

About 20 minutes into the conversation, Sayori, after helping me drain a few bottles of Suntory, asks me if I want the extended service. I ask her how much it is and what does it entail, although I'm pretty sure of both. She replies with the ¥12,000 figure and moves her hand in the motion of the international sign for a hand job. "That's a bit steep, isn't it?" I say in a very un-Japanese-like fashion.

"You think so?" says Sayori, taken aback. "Well at Hinomaru it's ¥12,000 for everything and they have *kuchi-sābisu* (blow jobs)," I explain. "But at Hinomaru they throw the customer out as soon as he comes, we don't do that here at London. You can stick around and have another cold one or two until your time's up," she says. "That's very nice. I appreciate the offer but I'm really not up to it tonight, if you know what I mean." "I'm sure with me you'd have no problem, I'm very skilled," she says with a sly grin, rubbing her hand on my upper thigh. "I'm sure you are," I say as I project an equally devilish smile.

The best way to handle these situations, I've learned, is not to act like a cheapskate. Like the strange johns who get off more on the talk than the act, I give her the money and explain to her I'm more interested in chit-chat than any hanky-panky tonight (after all I am doing research for a book). She shrugs her shoulders, a bit confused, but accepts the money nonetheless and says she'll be back in a minute. When she returns we continue our conversation. I'm curious to know why she doesn't perform oral sex on her customers, a routine that seems to be the house specialty at other cabarets and pink salons, such as Hinomaru.

"Well," she whispers in my ear, "I'm sure you're a nice fellow but as a rule I don't do *shakuhachi* (the bamboo flute) on foreigners...you know...AIDS." "But Japanese can have AIDS too," I interject. "Oh I know that. I ask my customers if they've been to Southeast Asia. If they say yes, I won't do it with them either unless they agree to wear a condom." "Well, any Japanese fellow you're dealing with could have contracted AIDS the previous night from some gaij*in* prostitute in Kabukicho, don't you think about that?" " Yes, that's true. I guess I just size them up."

I have had a few too many beers and want to chastise her for making such discriminations. "Well, soon Japanese are going to have to look at AIDS as not just a disease borne by foreigners," I say. Sayori nods her head. She doesn't seem the least bit offended by the tone and direction of the conversation, probably because we had been sharing jokes for a good 30 minutes before things turned serious.

The chunky woman in the next booth is still working on the inebriated chap whose trousers are around his ankles. He has his right hand on the woman's very ample backside. It's not an erotic sight in the least. I tell Sayori I've had enough to drink and must get back home to do some writing before I end up like the bloke in the next booth. She seems reluctant to send me on my way. She hands me her name card which also contains the cabaret's name and address. She bows as I turn around to get in the elevator. I step forward and give her a peck on the cheek, promising that I'll return one day when there's something else stiff in my trousers besides my empty wallet.

HEALTHY TOUCH

▼▼▼▼▼▼▼▼▼▼▼▼▼▼▼▼▼▼▼▼▼▼▼▼▼▼▼▼▼▼

Semantics are a requisite skill in determining the various shades of Tokyo's pink world. The English language, traditionalists argue, has been warped by the Japanese and words and phrases have taken on incomprehensible or hilarious meanings, books have been devoted to this phenomenon. The less orthodox among the *gaijin* understand that languages are organic and words and meanings change with the times and places. In Japan an English phrase adds a chic touch to a corporate image. Kanebo cosmetics for years has promised that its products are "For Beautiful Human Life." Yes, of course. Longtime residents mourn the passing of retired ad campaigns such as one Tokyo utility's evocation of "My Life, My Gas."

For the aficionados of the pink world the place to go for some decades was the Turkish bath or *toruko*. The one-on-one Bathing Industry Association (yes, even they are organized) finally heeded to complaints from the Turkish Embassy and in one fell swoop all *toruko* from Hokkaido to Okinawa became soaplands. Nothing else changed. They didn't even add bubbles to the bath. In recent years soaplands have gained some competition. Just as many young women in Japan now eschew the traditional postprandial bath for the morning shower and *asashan* shampoo, the pink industry has also seen a switch from the bath to the shower.

A visitor who has been away from Japan for some years is likely to scratch his head as he ponders the plethora of signs around the country advertising *fasshon herusu* (fashion health to the uncomprehending) or *herusu massāji* (health massage). The *fasshon herusu* and *herusu massāji* joints are not new-wave health clubs but a slightly less wet version of the old *toruko* and new soaplands. Most neighborhoods have such establishments tucked away in alleys and they are particularly abundant in the traditional entertainment districts of Ikebukero, Shinjuku, and Shibuya.

While Shinjuku's Kabukicho district is user-friendly for *gaijin*, the so-called health establishments of

Ikebukuro and Shibuya are less so. A survey of Shibuya's Dogenzaka area found only one establishment reluctantly willing to accept foreign (preferably North American or European white) clients. But the last laugh is on the *gaijin* who cough up the required ¥12,000 for the service. While the Japanese men will be given the normal treatment climaxing in oral service, the foreigners only get the hand job and there's no rebate for getting less than Suzuki-san in the next room is entitled to.

Foreigners desiring a more sensitive reception in the new health world should venture out to Koiwa, the last stop in Tokyo proper before the Edogawa River and Chiba Prefecture. There's more of a laid-back spirit out in Koiwa and the prices are cheaper than in central Tokyo because the area caters to a more down-scale clientele—the commuter making a solo stop on his way home to the far reaches of the bedroom communities in Chiba. A foreigner wandering the side streets around Koiwa Station is likely to run into a friendly tout who will steer him into a variety of locations. One barker even promises foreigners a frolic with a "geisha girl!" It is true they wear kimono but that's as authentic as the geisha bit gets. No visit to Koiwa should be considered complete without a visit to Banana House which has no compunctions about admitting foreigners—after all the whole staff is non-Japanese.

"Akemi" is one of the six Thais who work in the house. All are part-time workers. Akemi spends her mornings in beauty salon school, enrolled in a two-year course she hopes (with her earnings from Banana House) will allow her to open her own hair shop in Bangkok soon. The girls earn ¥10,000 per shift, working from one p.m. until midnight. Since they are not in

Japan as hostages of the establishment, as is the case in many places, there is a more relaxed and friendly atmosphere. The Thais of Banana House also speak more than rudimentary Japanese, making it a more pleasurable experience for Suzuki-san.

"Please take off everything," he hears soon after entering the two-mat-sized room with a small table, a coat hanger, and a cot-sized bed. Akemi has entered and already slipped out of her black dress and into a towel revealing that she has large breasts for an Asian woman. After the customer has disrobed, Akemi hands him a small red towel and leads him across the narrow hall to the shower stall. There's barely enough room for two inside and the wash pays particular attention to the genitals of the client. Passing initial inspection, Suzuki is toweled dry and led back to the room. Akemi sets a timer on the table (you've got 20 minutes guys) and removes her towel. She drops to her knees on the bed and begins licking his penis several times before asking if it's OK to place on the thin see-through condom. Suzuki shrugs his shoulder but not 15 seconds later Akemi asks him if he would like the genuine article. Suzuki is a bit confused because the tout made it clear that he'd be assured a blow job but no intercourse. "How much is the uh, real thing?" "Five thousand yen," Akemi replies. Suzuki has to decline. Like many salarymen he turns over his paycheck to his wife and he's just blown a week's allowance on everything leading up to the blow job. "Sorry I've only got ¥3,000 left and I need some of that to get back home." "That's too bad," replies Akemi who returns her skillful mouth to the condom. "May I touch you there," Suzuki says moving his hand up Akemi's thigh. The three beers at the *yakitori* stand with the guys from the personnel section have emboldened Suzuki to get all he can for his week's allowance. "Yes, it's OK," she says. He feels between Akemi's legs hoping he can get her a little wet.

Suzuki asks Akemi how old she is and gets a reply of 25. Actually she looks a few years older than that but Suzuki feels lucky to have drawn Akemi because of her breasts which seem more than twice the size of his wife's. Looking at Akemi's voluptuous body and succumbing to the extremely pleasant sensation of her mouth over his plastic-encased organ, Suzuki gives in to the inevitable with minutes to spare on the timer. Following the deft removal of the condom and a thorough wiping with a cold towel Suzuki is surprised to get an offer of a real massage from Akemi. Suzuki learns that a massage is more relaxing afterwards than before since a major amount of tension has already been released. As Akemi is about to lead the again clothed salaryman out the door she taps his crotch and says "When the Mrs. isn't taking care of you don't forget to come see me." Suzuki inwardly expresses surprise and emits a smile on the outside, wondering how she knows that he is married.

SUDS

▼▼▼▼▼▼▼▼▼▼▼▼▼▼▼▼▼▼▼▼▼▼▼▼▼▼▼

The faded *katakana* characters on the wall inside the entrance can still be read *toruko*, the Japanese word for Turkish bath. But alas, as we have learned, the *toruko* no longer exist. Thus this establishment, directly across from the designer police box in Shibuya, must be a soapland. The establishment, which bears no name on its exterior, has seen its better days. It appears to have faded along with the *toruko* characters. The senior citizen receptionist on the cavernous B1 level takes the patron's ¥4000 entrance fee, hands him a number, and directs him to wait on the tattered sofa. The other fellows waiting for their numbers to be called read newspapers or eye the fuzzy picture on the TV. There's no camaraderie among them and if one didn't know better the bored expression on their faces could indicate they were waiting for an appointment with their accountant.

Number six is greeted by a woman in a kind of outfit that seems more appropriate for a dental technician or a pharmacist. The lady appears to be well into her forties, perhaps in her fifties, a face and body with stocky legs not much different from the housewives to be found down the street shopping in the fruit section of the grocery shop. The pair enters a creaking elevator at least as old as the woman and it slowly makes the journey up a couple of floors. She tells the young man her name is Kimiko. She says little else except politely asking her third patron of the afternoon to undress and put his clothes in the basket after they enter the large room.

On one side of the room is a bath and a small sauna contraption. The other side has a tiny bed similar to what one would expect in a doctor's examining room. After undressing, the fellow is thoroughly hosed down, and then as he sits on a stool, is soaped from head to toe. Kimiko spends an inordinate amount of washing time on the genitals, giving the testicles a pleasant scrubbing as if they haven't been washed in weeks. Usually by this time the cock needs no prompting but Kimiko wants to

be sure it will have no trouble completing its mission down the road. "It's really quite big," she says with an admiring note in her voice. What's the appropriate reply the complimented fellow wonders? "Thanks for noticing" or "Aw, I bet you say that to all the guys"? After a rinsing it's into the hot bath for a relaxing soak. Kimiko is there to fiddle with the taps making sure the water is warm enough, but not too hot as to boil away the sensations. There's only a few minutes permitted in the tub because the meter is ticking.

Red as a lobster on stepping out of the bath the steaming body is toweled dry and led to the tiny bed. The fellow has his choice of desserts—talc or oil and then Kimiko goes to work applying years of experience to tired muscles. This massage alone is worth the price of admission. Even without paying for any extras the customer can be treated to a thorough massage and a professional hand job. This establishment tends to be more on the conservative side and, at first, the only extra apparently available involves paying for "double" service that results in Kimiko opening up her pharmacist's jacket revealing her small aging breasts and her pubic delta. Definitely nothing to write home about and certainly not worth an extra ¥4000 for this kind of peep show. For another few thousand yen, Kimiko announces, there's "double extra special" service which allows the already excited customer to touch her anywhere he'd like. In the old days for this price, Kimiko would have let him have his way with her. But this being a soapland across the street from a police station and with all these foreigners bringing AIDS into Japan, well, ¥12,000 just doesn't get you what it used to.

The experienced soapland patron knows that he

should be given a variety of options. A good soap lady puts her whole body into the job—stripping off her scanty uniform and climbing onto the table to give all of her customer's body a thorough grinding. Screwing may not always be permitted but at the very least one enjoyable and poetic option should be *tanima no shirayuri,* literally white lily in the valley. More graphically it means shooting your wad between her breasts. Who says the Japanese don't have a way with words?

4

▼▼▼▼▼▼▼▼▼▼▼▼▼▼▼▼▼▼▼▼▼▼▼▼▼

FULL SERVICE

CLUB NIKOL

▼▼▼▼▼▼▼▼▼▼▼▼▼▼▼▼▼▼▼▼▼▼▼▼▼▼▼▼▼

One wonderful aspect of the end of the bubble economy, the beginning of recession in Japan, and a strong yen, is that for foreigners living here, many nightspots, in order to survive, have begun opening their doors to customers they previously would have excluded. The diplomats, business executives with cost of living adjustments in their contracts, and locally hired foreigners for a myriad of high paying positions, has meant there are many thousands of *gaijin* walking the streets of Tokyo with lots of yen burning holes in their pockets.

The money is not usually the only thing in their pants yearning to escape. The horny fellows have no compunction about seeking instant gratification in exchange for cash. Club Nikol is one such establishment catering to such men. The nationalities of those gathered inside, employees and patrons, on a typical night could represent a goodly portion of the United Nations roster—Japanese, Chinese, Thai, American, and Peruvian are huddled in one corner.

The array of languages in use is an audio Tower of Babel. The hostesses banter among themselves mostly in Chinese and Thai. Back in the corner sits an inebriated American journalist, making comments about the size of the Thai girls' breasts in Spanish tainted with Mexican slang that is puzzling to the Peruvian diplomat. Meanwhile, a Taiwanese fellow with a huge jade circle dangling from his chest is crooning a *karaoke* tune in his Chinese dialect. Everyone uses heavily accented Japanese as a lingua franca, violating enough rules of grammar to have the Japanese hurrying out of earshot to the toilet, probably to puke at the sound of their native language being so thoroughly mangled.

Henri, the South American diplomat, is helping one of the Thai girls, Lit, celebrate her twenty-fourth birthday by nuzzling her shoulders and making crude analogies to big candles. The amply endowed young lady would be a candidate for top ranking in any beauty contest, except for the sad fact her family lacked money for an orthodontist to correct her prominent overbite. Lit is asking Henri whether he'd prefer to complete her birthday celebration with a sandwich. Henri doesn't appear to understand the meaning of the word, so Lit, marginally multilingual herself, at least when it comes to sex terms, airs both the French and Japanese slang. Henri, quite fluent in both, smiles and informs Lit he'd prefer just an old-fashioned one girl 69 routine. Now it's Lit's turn to beam. Soon she will call over Mama-san Hiroko, a Chinese woman in her late twenties, to present Henri with a ¥40,000 bill which will cover the flat all-you-can-swallow drinking tab (¥10,000) and the short-time "party" fee for which, at a nearby love hotel, she will engage in any of Henri's run-of-the-mill sexual proclivities for about 50 minutes, maybe a bit longer if she is still in the mood and he is still able to perform.

Nana, from Bangkok, had earlier been lavishing her attention on Henri, admiring his blazer patch and Kiwanis button. But seeing he has taken a shine to the woman in the establishment with the most dental enamel, if not cleavage, Nana turns to her right and begins to eye the other *farang*. It isn't long before Nana has convinced this sodden scrivener that he should be a good Yank and let her try on the small diamond earring displayed in his left lobe. I comply and hand over the small item. I expect that she will first remove one of her big golden earrings before trying it on. However, Nana wipes it on the *oshibori* on the table, warms it by rubbing it against her palm, slowly swirls it around the opening of her right ear canal for a moment and then, without so much as a flinch, uses the stem to make a new pierce in her lobe. "I'll give it back to you next time you come in," she says in Japanese. My jaw is agape, equally stunned by the deft surgical procedure and the audacious claim to temporary ownership of the diamond. But I had to admit it's a heck of way of guaranteeing the customer will have to come back a second time.

GOING TO THE DOGS

▼▼▼▼▼▼▼▼▼▼▼▼▼▼▼▼▼▼▼▼▼▼▼▼▼▼▼▼▼▼▼

Lek and another Thai girl are dozing on the sofa in the hostess bar where they work in Tokyo's Kabukicho red-light district. Sleeping next to them is their *yakuza* minder. It's one a.m. but business appears to be slow at Summer's Eve. The girls wake up and tell me they've only seen three customers the entire night. The punch-permed head of the gangster stirs and the man sleepily greets me. He remembers me from previous visits but isn't overly eager to see me again. Although I show up from time to time and shell out ¥10,000 for two hours of whiskey and chat, he can't recall me doing what most patrons are expected to do before the time limit expires—pay ¥30,000 for a quick tryst with one of the girls at a nearby love hotel

Lek and Eh are perfunctory in pouring me a *mizuwari*. "We're so tired because we have to work seven days a week," Lek says in halting Japanese. Lek says she came to Tokyo from Bangkok about 30 days ago under a three-month contract to the *yakuza*, brokered by her Thai boyfriend. They come from a country where it has been increasingly common even for girls in middle school to express desire to become prostitutes, with Japan being the preferred overseas assignment. The bank accounts full of yen accrued by their successful sisters and active recruiting by Japanese have turned the Don Muang–Narita airport run into a sex-trade shuttle. But there is also an economic downside to the business, not to mention the moral concerns. Many of the women are swindled by their *yakuza* handlers. Some of the Thais complain of arriving at Narita Airport already three million yen in debt to the mobsters for the cost of their passports and travel expenses. The women say that although food and board is provided they have to live off of any tips they receive until they settle their debts.

Thailand is not alone in exporting its daughters to Japan for sex. Taiwanese, Filipinas, and Koreans are also making the trek to Japan. When I ask Lek how she regards Japanese as patrons she gives me the same reply I've heard many times from other Southeast Asian women "Japanese are not so kind, but..." The sentence, in true Japanese fashion, usually isn't completed until they are sure of my nationality. "You're British?" Lek asks. "No, I'm American." "Americans are OK," Lek says, "But I really hate Arabs." Nearly every prostitute I have talked with in Tokyo has had some horror story to tell about a "date" with a foreigner, usually a Middle Easterner, an Iranian, or a Pakistani. The nationalities vary—I've even heard Yemen and Qatar—but the story is always the same, sex so brutal and violent that under different circumstances it would be legally prosecutable as rape.

During my initial visit to the place where Lek and Eh work I was greeted by six other Thai women, a Korean mama-san, the *yakuza* frontman, and the establishment's

mascot, a nervous miniature poodle named Peepee. To break the ice, I thought it would be a good idea to inform the group of what the dog's name means in English, *o-shiko* in Japanese). The joke went over like a lead brick. The *yakuza* did snicker a little, but the girls gazed at him blankly while the mama-san produced a weak smile.

My eyes dart from girl to girl. It seems one can almost tell how long they've been in the business by their faces. The most beautiful of the octet was Lek, who had a very listless demeanor. On the other end of the long sofa was the hetaera who was clearly the novice of the chorus of eight. With cropped hair, dowdy dress, and seemingly sincere smile toward the clients, she had to be the most recent arrival at Narita. Two of the Thai girls pour me another shot. I asked the mama-san how much Japanese the girls understand. "Not too much," she replied with the obvious. Mama-san calls little Peepee who goes into a begging routine standing on his back feet. "Would you like to date one of the girls or little Peepee?" she asks.

The mama-san then looks at her bevy and begins introducing the girls with their nicknames. "That's Banana, Orange, Peach, Persimmon, Tomato, Watermelon, Mango, and Papaya." Against my better judgement I burst out laughing. I feel I'm going to get the boot soon. My two hours and bottle of whiskey are nearly extinguished. Conversation is also nearing an end. Watermelon and Mango, sitting on the sofa across the room, are now clearly and rudely indicating that I'd better get something going or get going. Thai-accented Japanese-English words like *dēto* and *hoteru* are being flung at me. By this point a regular customer would have made a choice or chosen to leave solo long ago. A foreigner who asks too many questions and doesn't leave with a woman is obviously not good for business. I have learned that it is pointless to ask the prostitutes why they don't quit their jobs and do something else if they hate it so much. "*Shō ga nai,*" it can't be helped, is always the response even among the Thai women who speak almost no Japanese. It's an appropriate phrase all foreigners seem to learn very fast in Japan. The women talk of the need to provide money for their families. Women's help groups and some government officials in Bangkok and Manila decry the pervasiveness of prostitution in Thailand and the Philippines and the export of the young women in what critics call a white slave trade with Japan but no one seems to be providing an economic alternative. For the owners of the clubs, a lot of money can be made this way even much more than running a run-of-the-mill hostess bar. Not even counting the 20-50 percent they take from what the customers pay for take-out service, an average Kabukicho hole-in-the-wall front for prostitution can take in more than 120 million yen a year, according to police investigations.

It's not just individuals who are taking advantage of the relatively cheap sex for sale. Many of the bars, just like their more reputable hostess-type sister establishments, have corporate accounts. A police raid on Kabukicho's allegedly mob-run Chizuru turned up a list of 2,400 clients, according to the *Yomiuri Shimbun*. Among the customers in the black book were banks, construction companies, and several government officials. That in itself seems to be intimidating to the police who stage periodic raids on out-of-favor establishments. The next week and over on the next block, it's business as usual. A raided entity might take on a new name or move its staff and clientele to a new locale. And Tokyo has many such locales.

SEX ON A SOFA

▼▼▼▼▼▼▼▼▼▼▼▼▼▼▼▼▼▼▼▼▼▼▼▼▼▼▼▼▼▼▼

$ am has had a hard day in the office. The joint venture has been up and running for a year but there are still a lot of kinks to work out. The Japanese staff members are still scratching their heads over the daily barrage of faxes from the head office in Albany when Sam leaves for the day. Sam can't figure out why the local staff insists on translating everything for themselves although Sam's Japanese, perhaps still rudimentary, is good enough to always communicate the gist of the messages. Besides, there are two totally bilingual office ladies on the staff but somehow the men seem to have difficulty trusting their reliability in giving verbal translations. Instead everything gets sent over to the Japanese head office in Osaka by fax where it is translated and then wait a minute, you really don't want to hear about this. Even Sam is sick of it and instead of heading out with his Japanese counterparts to engage in the routine of *nemawashi* in smoke-filled snack bars singing off-key *karaoke* he decides to give himself a night on the town solo.

It has been a month (or maybe longer, Sam can't remember exactly) since his last roll in the sack. It had started out in a disco in Roppongi and Sam could tell right away that Sachiko had liked him. The only problem was she was with two of her other girlfriends from Chiba. So the foursome stayed together through the night, hopping from one dance spot to another, finally ending up around four a.m. in Pips. On the way in a very tall and very inebriated US marine had tried to make a grab at Sachiko. Sam defended her honor and averted (but barely) resorting to fisticuffs with the drunken jarhead.

Sam and Sachiko began making out at their table as the two other girls began dozing off, not holding up very well in their wait for the first train. After the lovebirds were able to ditch the girls at the subway station around five a.m., Sam asked Sachiko to breakfast in Roppongi. A couple of doughnuts later, as they were passing a love motel on Dogenzaka hill, Sam gently took Sachiko by the arm and steered her in. She did not resist.

Sam is remembering all of this as he is ejected from the Yamanote train at Shinjuku Station as part of the evening rush hour crowd. The all-night disco crawl had been exhausting. Sam had been up to those type of marathon sessions in pursuit of a good (or any) lay back in his college days but now as a professional expat (sort of, he doesn't get a full housing package like his buddy Milt who works for a British securities firm) he feels he shouldn't have to go through such a rigorous routine to answer his hormonic call. There has to be an easier way. Sam thinks he has found the answer. The other day at the American Pharmacy he picked up a book with a strange and tempting cover called the *Tokyo Pink Guide*. Skimming through it (skipping the history stuff up front) Sam had learned that he should be able to get laid in some fashion despite being a *gaijin* and having less than ¥20,000 in his pocket.

Coming out of the east exit of Shinjuku Station Sam heads down to Kabukicho. The Koma Theatre complex beckons him like some kind of radar beacon. About a block from the theatre stand a bunch of touts thrusting little flyers into the hands of passing men. When they see Sam is a *gaijin* they don't offer him anything. But one young fellow dressed in a cheap knockoff of an Italian suit does, addressing Sam in Japanese. "Hey brother, give this a try." Sam looks at the paper. It has a head shot of a cute young woman in a kimono. "¥11,000 for 40 minutes. Sex with a beautiful Japanese girl," the tout promises. "Too good to be true," Sam replies. "No, no it's true," insists the tout pointing to the kanji on the flyer. "Really it's sex. You can come one time. Nice *pitchi pitchi* girl." Sam thinks for a second and mutters to himself, "Ah, what the hell. What've I got to lose?" "Only ¥11,000 Sam!" shouts his wallet-minding conscience. "Okay, show me the way," Sam says to the tout.

The tout leads Sam over to the building housing the Naniwa Udon noodle shop on the first floor. Sam has no idea of the real name of the building. (If he had read the *Pink Guide* more thoroughly he'd know, as you do, that it's the Number 21 Tokyo Bldg.) Up to the tenth floor they go and Sam forks out ¥11,000. The tout smiles, thanks Sam, and leaves. Another young gentleman with a flashlight leads Sam to a sofa behind a thin see-through curtain and tells him politely to wait just a moment and someone will be with him. In the room, if you can call it that, a small TV on the table plays a pink movie featuring a supposed clandestine taping of a guy having sex with his girlfriend in a love hotel. Sam had rented a few of these kind of tapes from his local video store but he didn't enjoy them very much. They were always filled with sequences of women being tied up and whipped with badly acted moans that were supposed to denote a mixture of pleasure and pain. If it wasn't S&M there had to be a scene of vegetables being inserted in various female orifices. Sam wondered if the Japanese were really as kinky as suggested by the pink movies and the comic books the salarymen read on the trains.

A woman in a slinky nightgown enters the cubicle and closes the curtain although it is still possible to see out into the tiny hall. "Good evening, I'm Risa," the young lady says. Sam introduces himself, wondering if he also is supposed to use a fake name. Sam looks at her in the very dim light. If he had had a couple more drinks she would look pretty good, he thinks, although describing her as *pitchi pitchi* is a bit of an overstatement. She is no bright belle and her legs look like they've seen the senior half of their twenties. Well, anyway, Sam has paid his ¥11,000 and is determined to find out how far truth in advertising goes.

After bringing him a very watered-down *mizuwari*, Risa chats with Sam for a few minutes. Neither wants to waste too much time though, aware of the 40-minute limit. The usual pleasantries are exchanged. Sam is complimented on his Japanese and he explains honestly that he studied it at state college for a couple of years before coming to Japan. Sam finds out that Risa claims to be 23, living in Tokyo, but originally from Saitama. When Sam asks her about hobbies, she seems taken aback by the question before mentioning drinking and betting on horse races. They aren't exactly the types of activities Sam expected of a nice Japanese girl, but then again, perhaps Risa is not a nice Japanese girl.

"Well, how about taking it off," Risa finally says. Sam hesitates for a moment. He's not sure what to take off. And he isn't used to this kind of abrupt approach. Usually, Sam had most of a young lady's clothing removed before getting the first-time green light for further shedding on his part. Traditions carried over from the back seat of Chevys in high school are hard to break. Sam downs his drink and begins unbuttoning his shirt. Risa giggles. "No, it's kind of cold in here, you can leave your shirt on," she says. Sam is starting to have his doubts about whether he will be getting the sex for ¥11,000 the barker had promised. Sam switches gears and begins unbuckling his belt. Risa seems to relax and begins undoing her frilly getup.

When Sam's pants and underwear are finally down to his ankles Risa takes a damp *oshibori* to his genitals. Moving closer to him on the sofa she begins stroking him. "Hey, it's pretty big," she says. Japan is always good for the average *gaijin* guy's ego. "In America women have big breasts don't they?" Risa asks. "Well, some do, yes," Sam replies somewhat baffled by the casualness of the conversation as Risa continues to work on him. "I'm sorry but Japanese women have such small boobs," she says. "Quite all right. Women with small breasts seem to be more, uh, sensitive," Sam says searching for the proper term and finally resorting to the Japanese-English *senseeteebu*. "Hmm," says Risa with a pondering sound. "Are you about ready?" "Yeah, I think so," Sam replies, not sure what he is actually ready for but knowing he is ready for something further to happen. Risa reaches onto the table and breaks open a condom packet. Sam begins to go limp anticipating loss of feeling, and feels dissapointment, fearing she is going to attempt to give him a blow job with this thing on. But then matters quickly take a hopeful turn up. Risa removes her panties and says "you can do anything but don't touch me down there." Sam knows from his perusal of the *Pink Guide* that the removal of undergarments at this stage is not just for show. "Okay, let's do it," Risa says flipping off the TV before leaning back lengthwise on the sofa, and propping up her legs. Without the glow of the television it's too dark for Sam to skillfully maneuver. Risa lines up the essential elements and away they go. Sam silently thanks the barker ten floors below on the street for not giving him a bum steer.

SEX IN THE PARK

▼▼▼▼▼▼▼▼▼▼▼▼▼▼▼▼▼▼▼▼▼▼▼▼▼▼▼▼▼▼

Sex in the park has long been a pastime of lovers everywhere and Tokyo's Hibiya and Yoyogi parks are perennial favorites of Japanese couples. But the activities in Japan's Ise Shima National Park are perhaps unparalleled anywhere in the world. One portion of the park is Watakano Island, which many visitors—including the few foreigners who have dared to make the journey—will always remember as a licentious man's paradise.

The park is located on the Shima Hanto Peninsula on the eastern fringe of the region of Japan known as (no kidding) Kinki. For most visitors who take the train in from Nagoya or Osaka, it is the home of some of Japan's most sacred shrines and the tourist (and *gaijin*) friendly Mikimoto Pearl Island. Most tourist maps, however, make no mention of Watakano although it has been thriving as a guys' tourist destination by word of mouth for centuries. There's one very good reason for this that remains to this day—of the 450 residents of the island, nearly half are young women who spend most of their nights entertaining visiting men. Getting there, however, is not as easy as a phone call to the Japan Travel Bureau. It's a good bet that whoever handles your travel arrangements in Japan has never heard of the place.

For the foreign fellow who wants to make a visit the best procedure is to talk your favorite vice-loving Japanese buddy into making the journey with you and having him or a discrete soul make the mandatory reservations for you. The reason for this becomes clear soon after boarding the ferry for Watakano when it becomes obvious that someone besides the skipper is in charge. It doesn't take long to deduce that it's the no-nonsense fellow with the punch-permed hair who gives the passengers the once-over and asks for their names and lodges where they have reservations. The information is relayed by two-way radio and only after verification that everyone on board has a reservation does the ferry finally depart. There are apparently two types that are not welcome on the island—police detectives and reporters.

Fourteen lodges and inns dot the coast of the island which also features nearly two dozen "snack bars." At the check-in desks prospective patrons fill out a detailed card, again, apparently another attempt to root out cops and journalists who might ruin the fun for everyone. The female attendant who shows you to your room wastes no time with frivolities and immediately asks "What do you plan with the ladies tonight?" The fee system is the same at every establishment on the island. The lodge, at six p.m., hosts a welcoming party for which every guest is required to make a reservation. The "flower fee" is ¥16,000 for two hours. Your flower, in most cases, is supposed to be your partner for the night.

To see the flower really blossom you'll need to provide a little extra water—¥12,000 for 20 minutes and ¥20,000 for 45 minutes.

The overnight shift blooms at 11 p.m., several hours after the welcoming party ends giving guests time to store up energy for a second round or providing initial companionship for those who don't hit it off with their flower in the first session. The *tomari* all-nighters cost ¥40,000. To get around an obvious violation of the Anti-Prostitution Law the guests are not supposed to consummate the relationship in the lodge with the girls of their choice but must take them to a nearby love hotel. For the customers who decide to go for the pricey *tomari* they will not only enjoy a pillow companion for the entire night but will have a breakfast companion and someone to see them off at the ferry landing upon departure.

Others find it preferable to stroll the streets. The *yukata* is the dress of choice on the island. Wearing of the distinctive lodge *yukata* allows the various brothels to recognize where the visitors are staying and permits them to sign for payment for girls with the amount being put onto their bill back at the inn. As soon as a *yukata*-clad patron enters one of the snack bars he is asked what kind of woman he'd prefer to join him. Although the bar offers drinks and *karaoke* there's no need to stick around for booze and tunes after the woman meets you. Many will find themselves immediately being escorted to an adjacent love hotel.

The Japanese ladies of the night, who hail from the length of country—Hokkaido to Okinawa—say they prefer plying their trade on the island to a soapland close to home because they never meet acquaintances here.

Another big draw for the men and ladies alike is the seemingly autonomous rule on the island—there are no police, no official governing body, and allegedly no mobsters running the show either. But anarchy doesn't mean there are no rules. Smoking on the street is prohibited because there's no fire department. The ladies are prohibited from getting any fires burning too—meaning they cannot engage in a relationship with any man residing on the island.

As is the case with the pink world throughout Japan, foreign women are making inroads in the park. Many can be spotted looking out of the windows of their second-floor rooms above the bars and coffee shops. Most estimates show that there are 75 Thais and a few Filipinos on the island, many of them refugees from harsher treatment elsewhere in Japan. The foreigners report they are payed ¥100,000 per month no matter how many men they sleep with. Most are trying to pay off multi-million-yen "fees" that were extracted from

them by gangsters when they arrived in Japan to go to work. For them the island is a prison. They say that unless they pay off their debts they can't get their passports back and thus can't leave Japan. The mornings at the ferry launch are thus especially poignant. Perhaps the girl who sheds a tear as she waves goodbye to last night's john is wishing she too could board the boat.

5

▼▼▼▼▼▼▼▼▼▼▼▼▼▼▼▼▼▼▼▼▼▼▼▼▼

HOME DELIVERY

DIAL-A-MASSAGE

▼▼▼▼▼▼▼▼▼▼▼▼▼▼▼▼▼▼▼▼▼▼▼▼▼▼▼▼▼▼▼▼

It's two a.m. and Frank can't sleep. His Japanese girl friend of seven months is pressuring him for a "commitment" and he has told her perhaps they shouldn't see each other this week. The rumors out of the corporate headquarters in New York are of a hostile takeover. The Tokyo gravy train could soon be over for Frank. He doesn't give a damn. He's managed to squirrel away in his Sakura Bank account the equivalent of $75,000. Frank gets out of bed, throws on a robe, and opens a desk drawer in one of the other three rooms of his Yoyogi apartment. He glances at the clock and notices it's too late to order a pizza.

"What the heck," he mutters to the walls. Reaching into the drawer he picks at random one of the dozens of small flyers he's picked out of his mail slot over the past few months. All of the leaflets mention massages and list a phone number. There's the oil and powder massages. Various courses are offered with different types of girls. The prices for 60 minutes of massage vary between ¥11,000 and ¥17,000. Services are offered until four a.m.

Frank, with several beers under his belt from earlier in the evening, picks up the phone and thinks to himself that if he is capable of getting a pizza delivered he probably can have a woman show up at the door in 30 minutes or less. A man answers with a sharp *"moshi moshi."* Frank wonders what he should say to get the ball rolling. Using polite (but not too polite) Japanese, he says "Can I get a massage?" The voice requests his address, phone number, and name. Frank is then asked his nationality. "American," he replies. The man says he will call right back. Frank hangs up the phone and not 30 seconds later it rings. "Frank-san desu ka?" the man asks. He replies in the affirmative and the voice asks what he would like. "The 'A' course please," he says. The A course promises a young and slim girl. "Well right now all the A course girls are busy. How about a *guramā* girl?" he asks. Frank thinks a minute. A Japanese girl with big breasts might not be all bad but there could be a catch. "How much is it?" "It's normally ¥17,000 but..." "Ah, that's a bit much if she's not A course I think," Frank says, looking for an easy way out of this one. "Well in that case how about ¥15,000?" the voice asks. "She's not *debu* is she?" "No, no she's a little big but not *debu*. She's really a *pitchi pitchi* girl and she's in your neighborhood. If you don't like her you can just send her away." Frank relents, figuring that she can't be too much on the monstrous side—this being Japan—and after all he'll only have her for an hour, not for the rest of his life. "OK, send her over," Frank says.

Slightly less than 30 minutes later there's a soft knock on the door. Frank opens it and finds himself greeted by a young, short, but by no means skinny woman. Calling her fleshy would be overly kind. Frank has never had a fat woman in his life, especially a sizable Japanese lady.

Her hair is done up in curls in a style that was probably big among Missouri farm girls in the 1950s. She reminds Frank of a pig cartoon. Once inside she begins with an apology. "I'm sorry but we are required to get the money up front. He hands her ¥15,000 off the dining-room table he had set aside. "Thank you very much. I'm Sara. Now I must call in. May I use your phone?" she says. Frank nods his head and she makes a quick cryptic call. "Have you taken a shower?" she asks after hanging up the phone. "A shower? Why, yes I had one this morning." She giggles a bit. "Well you must take a shower first."

Frank climbs into the shower and soon there is a knock outside the bathroom door. "Excuse me, may I come in?" She enters and for the first time Frank has a real look at her. Put a few more pounds on her and she probably could enter into the *ōzeki* ranks of the sumo world. She is no beauty. There is a big hunk of flesh around her mid-section but she definitely has the largest tits he has ever seen on any Asian woman. Well, this will be one to share with the other *gaijin* guys in the office the next time they go out on the town.

Sara takes the soap in hands and makes a perfunctory attempt to soap Frank's back. She then wastes no time soaping up his cock while she gives it the once over. After toweling off they both head for the bedroom. "Is this your first time?" she asks. "Uh, yes," Frank replies. "I see. Oil or powder?" she asks as she rolls back the bedspread. Not wanting to stain the sheets he requests powder. Frank removes his towel and rolls over. Sara powders his back and gives him a couple of light smacks. "OK, turn over now." she commands. Frank thinks to himself that she's not planning to waste any time. She doesn't. "It's big," she says. Sara takes his slowly rising member between her hands. She does a brief massage of his balls and then takes him into her mouth. When she comes up for air Frank notices that a small thin condom has been placed on his prick. He is amazed to see it there since he did not feel her placing it on. Well, after all, this woman does have one remarkable skill. "Would you like me to stick a finger up you butt?" she asks after noticing that Frank doesn't appear to be getting too turned on by the experience. In all his 30 years, no one, except his proctologist has ever done that. Well, there's a first time for everything thinks Frank. "Let's try it and see what happens," he says. Sara takes another condom, slips it over her finger and places a bit of oil on top of it. The finger inside him is a pleasant sensation for about 30 seconds. Then Frank becomes worried that she might induce an enema rather than an orgasm. "Uh, that's enough of that," he says pointing to his butt. She withdraws, a slightly hurt look on her face.

"What would you like me to do?" she asks. He moves her into position on top of him but she shies away when his cock gets too close to her pussy. Frank has heard you can do anything with these massage girls except intercourse. Frank isn't too upset because he has no strong desire to screw her, just to get off and then get her hefty body off of him. A few more minutes of oral stimulation does the job and Frank comes. He gives it a seven on a scale of ten. Not bad, after all. Sara begins giggling. "Wow, that's a lot," she says truly admiring the amount of sperm gushing out. Frank's dick wiggles around and this sends Sara into squeals of laughter. Frank looks up and smiles at her. Either this girl is not quite jaded or I do possess some unique skills, Frank is thinking to himself. "You've never seen that before?" Frank asks her as he continues to make his prick prance about. "No. No, never," she says. Frank is tempted to ask her how many penises her naked body has gazed upon but decides it is probably not a good question to phrase. A few minutes later Sara is bundled back into her pile of clothes in which she is much better looking. She calls in again to check out and before putting on her shoes in the alcove hands Frank a name card reading only "Sara" and with a telephone number. "Don't hesitate to call and ask for me anytime," she says as she steps out in the early morning air. Frank heads back in and drops the card into the desk drawer.

A week later, on a cool night a little after midnight, Frank finds himself horny again. His girlfriend stopped by on Sunday afternoon and, of course, they ended up in the bedroom. But Sumiko in the sack has been less of a fulfilling erotic experience since she started getting so damn serious and dropping hints about matrimony. During the act Frank's mind wandered to the previous week's encounter with Sara causing him to lose his hard on more than once. Sumiko looked down in disappointment so Frank forced himself to conjure up an image of a Japanese girl he once knew many years ago—long and slender legs, a beatific smile with almost a boyish face. God, she was about as sexy as any woman he ever bedded, Frank recalled as he shot his wad.

A couple tumblers of vodka has Frank's hand reaching into the desk drawer again. A new card had been slipped in the box a few days previous. No alluring picture of Marilyn Monroe or cartoon characters on this one, just straight text. The newly opened Este More promises a choice of oil, powder, or shiatsu massages.

The phrases in the center of the flyer in no-holds barred Japanese tout "Lots of Beautiful Women!!" It also says that all the women are in their twenties. The price is ¥12,000 for 60 minutes. This time around, Frank, not worried about being brushed off merely because he's a *gaijin*, is a bit more forceful in his demands. "She'll be under 30 right?" he inquires. "Yep, this one I'm sending over is 22," the voice promises. "Okay, but she's not a *debu*, I'd like a girl with skinny legs and all. "This one is right up your alley," the voice insists in a calm manner. Unlike the last time this voice seems confident of himself. Frank has an intuitive feeling that this time indeed he may get what he'd like. The voice intimated in a phrase Frank didn't quite understand that extra service was available for an additional ¥5,700. Hmmm, this could turn out all right was Frank's thought as the doorbell rang no more than 15 minutes later.

Opening the door Frank is greeted by a tall woman with slender legs and a slightly boyish face. For a fraction of a second Frank is taken aback and his heart skips a beat. "There is a sex angel in heaven looking over me," Frank says to himself. Her name is Rei. She is the woman of Frank's dreams (at least physically). After he disrobes and lies with his back facing Rei she begins to work on him with her thumbs. She's no professional at shiatsu but at least she knows where the proper pressure points are. Rei, unlike Sara, takes her time to making it around to playing with his butt. Rei however has left on her shirt and her stockings. This is slightly unnerving to Frank because as Rei finally begins to bring his pecker to attention he is desiring a look at all of this wonderful body. Despite his gentle and polite request Rei is initially reluctant to fully disrobe. "It's cold," she says.

Frank who is stark naked and feels cool in a desert knows this is a lame excuse. He sits up and slowly lifts up her shirt. Finally she takes it off and asks "the bra too?" Frank nods his head and says "I'd like to see everything." "That'll cost you extra," Rei says as she removes the rest of her clothing.

Rei in the buff is everything Frank dreamed she should be. Her breasts will never win any contests but they are respectable by Japanese standards. She has shaved the majority of her pubic triangle leaving her pussy exposed. "You are really gorgeous," Frank tells Rei as he turns the table on her beginning to work on her sensitive parts. Rei, at first seems reluctant, but finally gives in and begins to emit moaning sounds. The sound effects get an A for effort but they're right out of those exaggerated Japanese porn movies that Frank has rented a couple of times from the neighborhood video store. Rei tries to keep her thighs together, finally relents but makes it clear that sex is out of the question at any price. Frank allows her to return to playing masseuse and Rei pulls out the oil and asks for some tissues from the box at the foot of the bed. When Frank comes a beatific smile shines on Rei's face. Yes sir, she does look just like that girl from some years ago. "You Americans really come for a long time," she says as she goes to work with the tissues. "Japanese don't?" "No, not as long as Americans." "I wonder why that is?" "I don't know," says Rei looking slightly perplexed. "But Americans seem to enjoy themselves more." "Yeh, we've made into a great tradition I guess." Rei laughs. "So Rei-san, you uh know about Americans?" "Yeh, a few. There was another guy in this apartment. Kinda tall but very quiet. He came for a long time." Frank figures it's the guy on the seventh floor who works for that big news wire service. The North American journalist types in Japan are the only group reputed among the *gaijin* crowd to be more lascivious and loose with their money than the European bankers.

Back in the main room as Rei is putting on her coat Frank puts two ten-thousand yen notes in her hand. "Sorry but it's ¥25,000," she says looking up at him with a smile. Knowing it would be bad form to argue and his only mistake tonight was not to put a price on her panties coming off, Frank reaches into his wallet and peels off five one-thousand yen bills.

6

STREET SCENE

STREETWALKERS

▼▼▼▼▼▼▼▼▼▼▼▼▼▼▼▼▼▼▼▼▼▼▼▼▼▼▼▼▼

One station west on the Chuo Line local train from Shinjuku is Okubo. In the numerous alleys behind the station are rows of love hotels, some with signs in Japanese reading "One Person OK." Love hotels are usually reserved for couples only, bring your own mate, but Okubo's have seen fit to bend the rules to cater to local conditions. Among the hotels several Latin-looking girls with red hair dart about on bicycles among the passing males. There's a lot of eye contact. Occassionally a girl stops her bike and asks one of the fellows in grammatically incorrect Japanese, "Wanna play?" The men always reply, "How much?" Bargaining ensues and the rock-bottom price usually quoted is ¥25,000. The Latinos, mostly from Colombia, on nights when the weather is better and the foot traffic is heavier, don't hesitate to ask for twice that amount. Sometimes a suit-clad salaryman is foolish enough to accede. That makes the Spanish-speaking girls of Okubo among the highest priced streetwalkers not only in Japan but, perhaps the world.

Down another one of the alleys stand a gaggle of Oriental girls, most speaking Thai. A john approaches one of them who looks less hardened. In Japanese he asks her where she's from. She slurs a reply that sounds like "Manila" but her accent is definitely not Tagalog. He politely asks her to repeat her answer. "Myanmar," is the clearer reply. "Oh Myanmar, Burma," he confirms. Her Japanese and Thai are practically non-existent. The Japanese customer obviously speaks no Burmese and a few words of English serve as a backup to her rudimentary Japanese. The prospective patron gets her down to ¥15,000 but he's not sure if she is clear on the demand that he desires to spend an entire hour with her. "Ichi-jikan daijobu desu ka?" he asks her, meaning "Is an hour OK?" "Ichi-man OK," she replies. She thought he was asking if ¥10,000 was all right. The Japanese john has just inadvertently accomplished a great bargain that would make any Afghan bazaar patron proud.

They enter one of the love hotels. The room is ¥2,500 for two hours, but none of the johns get to keep a girl around for that length of time. She tells him her real name is Pen. In Japan she goes by the nom de guerre of Aiko, meaning Love Child, a common name for girls. Pen is what traveling men in Asia call a "white tiger," a woman practically devoid of pubic hair except for a few thin strands. She says she is 20, which is probably correct. An uninitiated non-Asian would probably guess that such a girl would be about 12 or so because of the lack of pubes and her tiny breasts. But Pen is already wide around the girth for a young Asian woman. She may even have had a child back in her home country.

In between their couple of love-making sessions during their 50 minutes in bed, the temporarily sated businessman decides to do some geographical detective work. Where in Burma is she from? How did she get to Japan? All he can muster out of her is that she spent a few months in Thailand. Despite no previous experience in Japan with which to compare, he judges Pen to be good at sex for a young Asian streetwalker. He gives her a massage in gratitude. She teaches him a word in her dialect, *sambae*, "feels good." Pen lights a cigarette and asks if she can have a cola out of the little stocked refrigerator beside the bed. As he hands her the bottle, she pulls out an elaborate makeup case and begins to repaint her oval light-brown face. His hour is up.

KOGANECHO

▼▼▼▼▼▼▼▼▼▼▼▼▼▼▼▼▼▼▼▼▼▼▼▼▼▼▼▼

B elow the tracks, along the overpass at Koganecho in Yokohama, the tattered curtains of a small dark bar vibrate as the Keihin Kyuko train rumbles by. A Thai woman casts a shadow on the street where a solitary man passes by. She holds up her right index finger, denoting that she's available for ¥10,000. This time she doesn't get a taker. The man, tottering, and from the looks of his shabby attire, a day laborer, stumbles on glancing up at the signs in Japanese reading *O-shokuji dokoro* and *Taishū sakaba*. Despite the promises of food and drink, few are partaking in the numerous joints with their tiny counters and chairs under the rail tracks.

Another woman, perhaps Thai, wearing a miniskirt, pulls down her top and bares the upper part of her breasts as prospective johns walk by. In heavily accented Japanese she says *"ichi-man en."* It's ¥10,000 for 15 minutes. Most of the women who ply their trade out of the hovels say they find at least one taker a night.

Koganecho has had its ups and downs over the last six decades but in recent years the color pink has again begun to fade in this little-known neighborhood of sex. Most Yokohama residents, it seems, are not aware of its existence and those who do know about it try to avoid it on their way home. Like Tokyo's Golden Gai district in Shinjuku, Koganecho to many passersby is an unwelcome reminder of an earlier era of wood and thin soup when a few yen was a lot of money. Also, like it's cousin Golden Gai, this neighborhood too is quickly disappearing and only a few seem to regret it.

Those with a taste for nostalgia are confident that Koganecho will survive in the face of adversity. After all it was calamity that gave it birth. After World War Two Koganecho became a site temporarily housing those burned out of nearby neighborhoods by the American air raids. As fortunes revived for the homeless, the ramshackle housing was generally converted into small shops, some of which still remain.

Stop in the ramen shop under the overpass for the full history lesson. The proprietor, Saburo Hattori, has seen a lot of changes along the street since the mid-forties. After the war, he opened Koganecho's first snack bar, employing a half-dozen hostesses. He contends that there was no intention to turn the neighborhood into a red-light district. "We started out as an ordinary bar," he recalls. "But a war widow took a shine to one of the regulars and began sleeping with him for money. Those were desperate times you know." From one fallen widow, a thriving enterprise was created and by the early fifties Koganecho was an established red-light district. Back then the going rate for 20 minutes of "play" was ¥200-300 and 45 minutes could be had for ¥500-600—about double the average daily wage! The glory days lasted until 1958 when Japan officially put the kibosh on prostitution. "That year most everybody closed down except for ten or so bars. They were selling booze, not girls, but by the following year it was pretty freewheeling again," Hattori remembers. And Koganecho went from boom to bust to boom—between 150 and 200 girlie bars competed along a 1,200-foot stretch. The futons on the second floors did a booming business.

The bursting of Japan's bubble economy has brought another bust though. Just ask Maya from Taiwan. Things were going so well for her in the neighborhood a couple of years ago that at the age of 30 she was able to begin running her own shop. It was only in the late eighties that foreigners were permitted to begin selling spring in Koganecho. With a lack of local talent on the base paths for home-run hitting, the nightspots of the neighborhood agreed that they'd steal an idea from Japan's pro baseball teams and set a quota for *gaijin* helpers. Each shop was permitted to hire one foreign girl. Many, like Maya (not her real name, of course), came from Taiwan, learned a little Japanese, found a native to marry on paper, secured a visa, and began working as mama-sans while paying ¥50,000 a month to their supposed husbands. At the peak, right before the bursting of the bubble economy, Maya says she was sleeping with ten men a night. By mid-1992 though, business bottomed out and Maya was lucky to snare one guy an evening. She decided to give up her shop and return to being a part-time employee. "There weren't a lot of customers anymore, my body was worn out and the rent became too high. So I quit. What a relief."

Foreigners who are used to facing discrimination in finding housing in Japan can sympathize with the *gaijin* women of Koganecho. Japanese who rent directly from the landlords pay ¥100,000 a month to lease a shop. The foreigners find that they're not able to rent directly and must sublet their tiny bars for ¥450,000 to ¥700,000 a month. Maya's compatriots aren't following her to the neighborhood these days. Now it's non-Japanese-speaking Thais—some in their teens—who are eager to take Maya's place. They usually work about three months in the area before moving on, quickly realizing that a girl with a little bit of talent and looks can do a lot better on the other side of the tracks.

Hattori, who doesn't seem to regret that he's now slinging ramen instead of bossing a bevy of beauties like he used to in the glory days, decries the changes. Not only have the women changed, but the men too, he contends. "The guys nowadays don't even want to have a drink first. In the old days a fellow would sweet-talk a lady before asking if he could accompany her upstairs. That art is lost," bemoans Hattori. "Now it's instant boom, 1,2,3—the guys say 'How 'bout it baby?' and the girls reply right away, 'OK'."

For years the hankypanky in Koganecho seemed to be OK with the cops. But with the influx of *gaijin* women making it very obvious about what's going on under the tracks, the Kanagawa Prefectural Police have been moving in, further driving away the life source of the neighborhood. In 1991 officers arrested more than 150 foreign women in Koganecho—most of them Thais. The police raids in subsequent years haven't relented. But the women here say they fear AIDS more than the cops. Koganecho reported its first case in the autumn of 1990 when an arrested Thai woman tested HIV positive. The women say they now insist that all customers use condoms. The younger guys comply but many of the older men refuse. They want it to be like the good 'ol days. But a look up and down the street reveals those days are gone.

7

▼▼▼▼▼▼▼▼▼▼▼▼▼▼▼▼▼▼▼▼▼▼▼▼▼▼▼▼

GEISHA

Sachiko & her

AMAZING

ANKLES!

CENSORED   CENSORED

SHOW
TIMES:
11:00
2:40
3:17

NOT FOR THE FAINT OF HEART!!

THE
GAIJIN'S ULTIMATE
FANTASY

▼▼▼▼▼▼▼▼▼▼▼▼▼▼▼▼▼▼▼▼▼▼▼▼▼▼▼▼▼

Bedding a geisha is no doubt the ultimate medal a male foreigner in Japan can earn. It is not only a rare prize because of the scarcity of bona fide geisha nowadays (between ten thousand and fifteen thousand by most estimates) but because it is considered a given by naive relatives and friends back home that any fellow worth his salt has had a geisha experience in Japan. Of course your Uncle Ralph back home in Reading has been brainwashed by those early 1950s Hollywood movies and *ukiyo-e* cocktail coasters to believe that geisha abound in Japan and are any man's for the asking. Any man who has been in Japan more than a day knows that not only are geisha scarce but they are expensive. On top of that, even if one walks through Tokyo's Akasaka district or the refined Gion quarter of Kyoto with a million yen to burn he would still have no guarantee of spending the night with a geisha.

But for those who truly yearn to fulfill this fantasy it can be done. The first step, of course, is to actually meet a geisha. Even if your language and navigational skills were sophisticated enough to locate what you thought was a geisha house in Akasaka (where most of the few authentic Tokyo geisha still travel to work by rickshaw) you would be barred entry unless you were with a longtime Japanese patron. If your business entrees involve dealings with the upper echelons of management of Japan's most presitigious companies (such as leading trading companies, multi-national conglomerates, or famous appliance makers) or members of the prime minister's cabinet you are probably in luck. If you broach the subject to your Japanese counterpart he will likely be more than happy to see that you get started.

It's likely that your introduction to the geisha will extinguish any sexual desires for them. Most geisha you will be dealing with will be well near retirement age. You will be wondering why your counterpart is beaming as the grandmotherly figure pours saké, occassionally takes to a stage to sing a ballad, pluck at a strange-looking instrument, or performs an esoteric dance. You will be puzzled although your intoxicated companion assures you that the woman is extremely talented. Unless you have been raised in Japan, all of this would be lost on you and you are likely to be more stimulated watching Kabuki.

Let us say that among the geisha at the party is a woman who looks below the age of someone who should be collecting her pension and strikes your fancy. Now what? Wire home for an early withdrawal of your retirement account fund. You are going to need it. Send a separate wire to the wife and kids that negotiations are going poorly on this trip and you can be expected to remain in Japan for the next six months to a year. You are going to need it. Your mission now along the road to your Herculean goal is to convince the youngish geisha that you are going to be her *danna* (master).

At some point along the way the geisha is going to have to generally like you, if not fall in love with you. Don't expect even the "like a lot" business to occur unless you appear on a regular basis (plan on a minimum expense of ¥100,000 per visit), charm her with your personality and gradually make it clear that you are willing to invest the equivalent of the GNP of Ghana on her over the next year or so. The fact that you are a *gaijin*, the one part of the equation you cannot alter, is likely to prevent her from seriously considering your offer of *danna*-ship. Then again, you never know, it could happen. And you could win the Publishers' Clearinghouse Sweepstakes too? Try it, you could already be a winner.

For the rest of us chaps who have no illusions of becoming a geisha's *danna*, there is, believe it or not, actually hope. In fact, by following the process about to be outlined here, the next time you see Uncle Ralph and he cracks that evergreen "Well, d'you get yourself a gee-sha girl yet in Toh-kee-oh?" you will be able to reply, "Yep, certainly did, as a matter of fact." I know it can be done. I did it. Of course, we have to enter into a gentleman's agreement and perhaps bend the rules slightly about just what exactly constitutes a geisha.

Among a group of expatriate journalists (what more knowledgable and esteemed jury could you ask for?) meeting one wet night at the Foreign Correspondents' Club of Japan, the modified standard was agreed upon. The standard Japanese definition of a geisha has always been hazy anyway. In the olden days in Kyoto, a geisha would first have to go through a long apprenticeship mastering the traditional arts; first serving as an apprentice *maiko* before she could wear the title and kimono of a *geiko*, the proper term for what were considered full-fledged geisha. However, in other places and times, the standards have been less rigid. But our panel of highly reputable scribes agreed that it would be unfair to consider as geisha just any woman wearing a kimono and pouring saké. After many hours of discussion lasting well past last call, a compromise was reached. A geisha, for our purposes, would be considered a woman who was a member of an officially registered geisha *kenban* (union or bureau) working in a traditional Japanese environment (tatami essential) and who has mastered one of the traditional geisha arts—dance, shamisen, or koto playing, or is taking certified lessons from a senior geisha in such skills. This definition conveniently took in the world of the *onsen* geisha.

Onsen means hot springs and Japan's steamy resort areas abound with recognized geisha who make appearances at group parties usually paid for by companies or groups of wealthy old friends on holiday. I had had the good fortune of attending such an event and thus had my entrée into the geisha world. I left the press club table that night knowing that I alone could claim the honor, although when you hear the full story you may demand that I rescind the claim on the basis of turpitude and chtuzpah.

Her name was Kiharu and I found everything about her fetching. But there was nothing obvious that revealed she was a geisha except for the upswept mound of hair atop her head. Dressed in blue jeans she did not walk in the slow graceful manner of a geisha and the look in her eyes was that of a woman who had spent time beyond the mountains of the Hakone hot-springs resorts. But the geisha Kiharu was hardly a woman of the world. Once she uttered the first words I heard her speak in English it became obvious where she had suffered the dilution of her Japaneseness. "How do you do," she said upon introduction inside the offices of the Yumoto District Geisha Union. Her words in English conjured up images not of saké and ukiyo-e but of moonshine, gators in the swamp, and four-wheel-drive pickup trucks with gun racks behind the seat. It was an American southern accent but not the refined diction heard in Nashville or Atlanta. My guess was L.A.—Lower Alabama. "That's a pretty good guess. I spent four years at the University of Southern Alabama," she said in a tone that revealed neither pride nor embarrassment.

My pal Mike Millard, a jovial newsweekly magazine editor (who, for some reason, keeps making appearances in other books on related subjects), had coaxed me out to his home base an hour's bullet-train ride from Tokyo to give me a grand tour of some of the few remaining authentic geisha habitats. During a late night three-way discussion with Wild Mike, myself, and Kiharu in the dining room of the Oan Resort Hotel it became manifestly evident that our young geisha had received less than adequate schooling in Alabama considering she had supposedly earned a B.A. in psychology. "Those letters Freud and Jung exchanged are really interesting," Wild Mike said, skillfully maneuvering his chopsticks in some strange rice and egg concoction. We had steered the conversation to the subject of the good doctors in an effort to hear more from the lips of our geisha belle. "Who's Jung?" the geisha with the alleged psych. degree asked.

"Karl Jung, the father of Jungian psychology, of

course," Mike said with a big smile. "Jung, I ain't never heard uh him," Kiharu said. Mike and I looked at each other, obviously telegraphing the same thought—what the hell did she do at the U of SA to earn that degree?

In her blue kimono it was easy to forget that this young lady had spent years in the cultural netherland of Mobile, Alabama being pawed by backwoods boys whose limited wits or Daddy's savings had taken them to a campus with a dubious scholastic reputation. Kiharu was a sure bet to be lusted after by men of any region, including those of the American Deep South. She stood five foot nine with long legs, a beautiful not-too-round face, and breasts that were much larger than average for a Japanese woman.

The last attribute I finally confirmed several days later when we bumped into each other during the annual Hakone Daimyo Festival, featuring hundreds of modern-day costumed samurai and authentic geisha in full regalia parading through the streets of the little mountain resort town near Odawara. Kiharu, dressed in a tight sweater and jeans, spotted me as I was walking backwards in front of the huge procession, snapping photographs. The head of the geisha union, elderly Mr. Nakayama, had given me his emblazoned *happi* coat which allowed me to march in the procession unhindered by the police and other minders trying to keep the audience behind a rope being carried along the parade route. I didn't recognize her at first. Her hair was different. "Yeh, I couldn't get it fixed in time to march with the geisha," she said. Kiharu was attached to the House of Twins, one of the two-dozen or so institutions supplying geisha to parties, hotels, and hostess clubs in the area. Each house was headed by an older woman who had worked as a geisha in her younger days and thanks to many years of frugal saving or the generosity of a wealthy patron was now in business for herself. Although Wild Mike and I had become popular among the younger geisha, the mama-sans did not take a shine to us. Too many of their girls had begun spending time with us off the meter and the old women thought it was costing them money.

That was hardly the case. A "beep beep beep" frequently interrupted our liaisons with the girls inside the retired geisha Sakon's little bar in Yumoto and a kimono-clad woman would reach inside her obi sash and pull out her pager. Then she'd shuffle to the telephone behind the bar to find out where she was being dispatched. Kindly Mr. Nakayama had given us practically free reign to enjoy the geisha in what Mike and I considered to be overly profuse thanks for the articles we had done highlighting his revival of Japan's geisha industry. Nakayama's introduction of such innovations for his union members as pension plans, paid overseas vacations, and even child care had lured women back into the business. Many, even now, shunned boring jobs in offices serving tea and shuffling papers to enjoy the handsome wages and greater independence available to a geisha.

The Yumoto District Geisha Union does not award the highest level of geisha-hood before the age of 30 and then only after the mastering of a traditional geisha art—such as playing a musical instrument or learning how to dance traditional numbers. By this age, they also had to master the other traditional arts—witty conversation and pouring drinks or a lewd combination of both, such as asking a patron to try *wakamezake*, literally sprout rice wine. A "yes" reply might allow one to indulge in saké-sweetened cunnilingus between a parted kimono.

Publically, however, even such novitiates as Kiharu, who still had trouble walking in a kimono, are considered geisha by the union, the girls themselves, and the customers. It seemed unlikely that Kiharu would ever achieve the highest level. She seemed to lack the dedication to pursue the refined arts. After only a few months on the job she was already looking for other work, despite making several hundred thousand yen per month in her present profession. "I've had an offer to work for United Parcel Service at Narita Airport," she announced to Mike and I as if this would be an appropriate career path for a young geisha with a psychology degree from a second-rate school in the American Deep South. Well, maybe it was. "That'd be uh, interesting," Mike said with a forced grin while searching for a more truthful reply. Wild Mike had his eye on the young Kiharu but by default she was, at least temporarily, mine, being as it was that she was seated to my right and Mike was the center of attention of a more Japanized young geisha, Ikemi.

Wild Mike, for months, had been making a half-hearted attempt to lure the lovely Ikemi away from her do-nothing, dim-witted boyfriend even the politest of Japanese in the bar usually referred to by his nickname of Dumbo. The Japanese were quite familiar with the Disney elephant with ears so big that he could fly. The human Dumbo of Yumoto was also cursed with such appendages. Mike would become increasingly bold with Ikemi in direct proportion to the number of beers he had consumed. Ikemi never seemed to discourage

these advances, making sure, as a good geisha should, to keep his beer glass always full. The staff of Asano and all the regulars of Sakon's humble establishment were in their own ways encouraging Ikemi to allow herself to be seduced by Wild Mike. Even though he was a *gaijin*, and thus an unusual romantic match for a Hakone geisha, he was kindhearted, humorous, and relatively well-off to boot. The wise old geisha knew that for such romantic pairings matters of race should perhaps be overlooked, especially when comparing the *gaijin* Mike to the good-for-nothing Japanese Dumbo. Mike knew this but resisted taking Ikemi. Yumoto was a small town and Asano his favorite drinking spot. If Mike consummated the relationship it would not be so easy to keep Ikemi at bay and it would likely put a severe crimp in any other potential extracurricular activities in the neighborhood. "Isn't she just wonderful?" Mike exclaimed as he implored her to teach him a new phrase in Japanese: "Please take your clothes off." Wild Mike then jokingly tried it out on nearly every woman in the place. The elderly elfin Sakon playfully slapped him on the shoulder and told him he was *sukebe*, lewd. Another geisha teasingly began to loosen her kimono revealing some skin around the shoulder.

Kiharu perked up and asked Mike "Where'd you learn to say that?" Kiharu and I had been in deep conversation comparing Hakone and Tokyo. She had never spent much time in the capital, a situation I'd begin to rectify a few hours later with a tour of Golden Gai. It was, of course, all part of a strategy to have her end up at my place in the wee hours of the morning in an area that was a mighty expensive cab ride from her home.

Seven hours after Kiharu and I bid good night to Mike and Ikemi, she began undressing without any provocation on my part. My confidence in asking her home peaked considerably back at Asano during a joke I was retelling. I had previously told it in Japanese in another bar and had received some good laughs, but this time I wanted Kiharu to translate since her language skills were far superior to mine. The joke involves an American man with a very small penis who flies to an experimental clinic in Switzerland for a transplant where he is shown progressively larger model organs (the unabridged version would take up several pages of precious paper). The punch line comes when the good doctor drags out a 12-incher and the fellow says "Yes, that's the one I want, but do you happen to have it in white?" During the course of trying to convert these measurements into metric, Kiharu explained that an 8-incher must be about average for Americans because she had never seen one smaller than that. This was another seminal moment when Mike and I telegraphed knowing looks, both of us obviously thinking this girl's math might be off but she's obviously held a few rulers in her hand. Now the day had added up to a nice score. Kiharu and I were in my bed and I wanted to find out how I'd measure up. By any man's standards, Kiharu in the nude had a very nice body, I thought as she began to purr. The climax to the whole saga came not with any orgasm but shortly before when she exclaimed, in that Lower Alabama accent, matter of factly during foreplay, "put it in." I stifled a burst of laughter and did as I was told.

8

LADIES ONLY

HOST BARS

▼▼▼▼▼▼▼▼▼▼▼▼▼▼▼▼▼▼▼▼▼▼▼▼▼▼▼▼▼▼▼

They are called *tsubame*, swallows. In the west we call them gigolos and Tokyo, never a city to miss importing any fad, has embraced them too. Tokyo, being primarily a man's city, is filled with more hostesses than hosts. But the city has long played host to legions of men willing to give their time and shed their clothes in exchange for money from women. For years there were discrete businesses willing to send a charming young fellow to a lady's door. For a long time, the clients were usually wives of rich men no longer willing to pay sexual attention to their spouses or hostesses who had no qualms with such matter of fact transactions involving money and sex. Nowadays even the office ladies are getting into the act but it's not usually just straight sex they're after. They are paying for men to take them on a drive, on a shopping spree, or escort them to parties.

The newest trend is to select a fellow outside of one of the host clubs (more on these spots later). The young lady is met by a representative of a group of gigolos at a coffee shop. He is immediately recognizable by his tanned thirties looks and a gaudy gold chain around his neck. He is carrying a notebook which includes pictures and short bios about the companions his firm can offer. The standard course that most women select includes a four-hour session of dinner and a romantic drive for ¥40,000. Most of the available men in their twenties are students at such renowned universities as Keio, Sophia, and Waseda. In the slightly older age bracket there is a wide selection of salarymen and those who run their own businesses. Most of the salarymen are married and work for such high-profile firms as JR, Asahi, Toyota, and Sony. There is only one admonition the representative gives to the prospective clients before their dates, "You can just about ask for anything but don't look at your host as a potential husband. They are just doing a job." The women are responsible for paying for meals and transportation costs, such as gas. Yes, it is made clear by the representative, sex is definitely an option for an extra ¥30,000 an hour.

For those women who like to see their hosts in the flesh before making an outside date with them there are several host clubs in Tokyo. The most popular and largest are the twin clubs in Shinjuku's Kabukicho district known as Club Ai and Club New Ai. Between them the two clubs boast a staff of three hundred men. Others in Kabukicho, in the minor leagues by comparison to the Ai twins, are New Cat's Eye with 40 hosts and Yoru no Teio with about the same number.

For a peek inside Club Ai, I dispatched an American journalistic colleague of mine, a fluent Japanese speaker in her late twenties with long straight blonde hair, a charming personality, and a great figure. I figured she'd be able to captivate the attention of the hosts and milk them for all the information required for this chapter. Here's what Kim found out.

Club Ai is not only the largest male host club in Shinjuku, it is the biggest in Japan in terms of space as well as the number of men. There are 60 men per shift: six p.m. until midnight and midnight until six a.m. Most of the hosts are in their late twenties and early thirties but the ages actually run the gamut from 18 to 56. Club Ai has a special ¥10,000 service-charge for first-time visitors. For that price you get some smelly fishy snacks, a few peanuts, five small bottles of mineral water, and one bottle of cheap whiskey. After you have been to the club once you become a full-fledged member customer which means you really have to pay. The cheapest bottle-keep charge is ¥10,000 with the average being ¥18,000. The really big spenders have them uncap a ¥500,000 bottle of special Hennessy cognac. The average bill is ¥50,000 to ¥70,000 for one and ¥70,000 to ¥80,000 for two women. Favored customers enjoy a so-called service discount from the club which usually amounts to only ¥10,000 off the regular price. This, obviously, is not a cheap spot, but remember that at all times you are surrounded by a minimum of three men.

Usually the festivities begin with three to five men sitting across the table from the woman or women. But as the night goes on the hosts will make their moves and actually sit on the couch with the female customer. This is meant to be a sign from the host to the customer that he enjoys her. All of the women want someone to end up on the couch with them by the end of the night. Besides the drinking and the conversation the big activity in the club is ballroom dancing to the music of live bands. All of the men are great dancers. On my first night I ended up with what I considered a somewhat old but supposedly successful host—a 45-year-old with fish breath telling me in child-like English while he pointed between his legs that "this is a pen." I answered in Japanese, "No it's not, it's your dick." Old Fish Breath was the only man who dared sit on the couch with me, however. The men, all well-groomed, are all wearing designer suits, most are in black but a few go for the Versace or Versace-like suits. All of the guys are attractive, but I would say that only four out of the 60 on the floor could be described as stunning, hot, or even model-like. That means the odds are not good of getting one of the top guys on the couch with you. A lot of the men appeared feminine—at least for my tastes—but according to one of the staff members there are no homosexuals working at Club Ai.

I made a date with one of the better-looking fellows to meet me for dinner one evening. Mr. T, as he prefers to be called, arrived for our appointment looking just as you would imagine a gigolo to look—a heavy fringed jean jacket with black suede patches and tight blue jeans with matching black suede patches. I could smell him coming from across the room. His gold Tiffany watch was blinding when it caught the light. Mr. T is 23 and came to Tokyo from Hokkaido five years ago to attend a good university but he quit after his first semester and gave it all up to become a geisha boy. He says he first started to raise money to open his own business, but then "once you get in it's hard to get out." He points out the example of a 56-year-old colleague with a family. Mr. T started as a pub host in Saitama Prefecture and worked his way up to the major leagues of Kabukicho.

He has worked for Club Ai for more than three years and has never once been paid a salary. Asked how he survives, he replies, "By dating." All of the hosts "date," some turning tricks quicker than others but Mr. T claims he has only "dated" once on the first meeting. He says it usually takes him two to three months after meeting an interested woman before his first date. "It is important to establish rapport with the customer, but also if I keep her coming back to see me at work, the club makes more money." Some hosts will date on the first night but most try to establish some kind of relationship before the sex begins. Mr. T says he believes that 50 percent of the women who come into his club are looking to sleep with a man on that night but only about five percent of them get their wish either because it is too late or they don't bluntly ask for their wish. If they are not bold, Mr. T says, most hosts will not pursue it on the first night. Mr. T says that a host must look good and must make the woman feel comfortable with him. When she feels comfortable is when she can begin to imagine making love with him and that's when the fantasy can turn into reality. The price for the evening outside the club is always determined before the date. The low end, (as is the case with the aforementioned service Steven mentioned), is ¥30,000. But most women are apt to end up peeling off ¥50,000 to ¥80,000 from their purses and providing perks—shopping and presents. Presents for hosts are so rampant and categorized among themselves that Mr. T can reel off the prices of different types of Rolex watches. He has three Rolexes, a Bulgari, a Tiffany, and a Pierre Cardin. He says that 20 of his co-workers have the top of the line gold, diamond-studded Rolexes. Mr. T hasn't earned his yet but he shares that goal with other hosts because that model is considered the ultimate gift from a lady. "Yes, I am materialistic. I want to look good and have nice clothes and accessories," he says.

Hosts typically do not get much respect in Japanese society, but if they look good they know they will at least merit a little bit of admiration if not respect. "We are professionals and we take pride in our work. We have ethics too which is why we rarely date on the first meeting," he explains. But there is a flip side to it that he readily acknowledges. "Hosting looks like a clean profession and I make it sound nice but it is dirty just like crime and drugs are dirty. Look, we are all doing it for the money," he says in a matter of fact voice.

Many women who have never ventured into a host bar or spent the night with a gigolo might be surprised to hear Mr. T boast that he has never worn a condom. He says he gets an AIDS test twice a year, which he claims is a lot more often that any of the other hosts. Testing is not mandatory and there is no education regarding AIDS from the clubs. "We believe that we are safe from AIDS if we avoid dating foreign women," he says. "We all have a *gaijin* complex." Mr. T says he has asked around the clubs to see if anyone would be interested in dating a Western woman but so far the responses have been negative. Although he adds that if a foreign woman is willing to establish some rapport with a host over a three to four month period then maybe they could "date."

9

THE GAY SCENE

FUNDOSHI NIGHT

FASHION SHOW: 9 to 9:30
WRESTLING: 10 to 11:30

FOR THE BOYS:
SHINJUKU 2-CHOME

▼▼▼▼▼▼▼▼▼▼▼▼▼▼▼▼▼▼▼▼▼▼▼▼▼▼▼▼

To any student of Japanese history the proliferation of gay bars in Tokyo will come as no surprise. Japan, after all, has a long history of tolerating, and at times glorifying, homosexuality. In the middle ages in Japan, homosexuality was rampant. It was considered a matter of course that acolytes and young novices in Buddhist monasteries were not only instructed in spiritual but physical matters by their teachers who had forsworn the intimacies of women. Although homosexuality appears to be the only sexual practice expressly forbidden by Tantric Buddhism it has been openly tolerated by most Buddhist sects throughout Asia—especially rampant in Korea, China, and Japan. In Tibet, a monk who openly professed his preference for fellow males was praised as enlightened because it meant he had overcome his desire for women! Obviously for someone who had never had natural inclinations toward heterosexuality in the first place this path to enlightenment came much easier.

Historians credit ninth-century Buddhist monks

with introducing homosexuality to Japan. It found a wide following in subsequent centuries. Despite phobias by present day Western militaries about tolerating homosexuality among their ranks most cultures witnessed a link between the martial arts and homosexuality. Japan was no exception. The samurai's code of *bushidō* included a healthy respect for *nanshoku*, male lust. Among the super-macho, after all, desiring a woman was seen as a weakness. The normal outlet was to take a young man or a boy as a lover.

The fourteenth-century shogun Ashikaga Yoshimitsu perhaps ranks as one of Japan's all-time great homosexuals. Under his patronage and futon twelve-year-old Zeami became a great Noh actor and developed the art form into the style it is known for today. A few centuries later when women were barred from the Kabuki stage their eager replacements were generally not mere cross dressers but effeminate men who saw nothing wrong in going home with their male groupies. During the Edo era it was not only from the stages that a man could find a same-sex lover. Brothels flourished providing young men, and those desiring even younger flesh flocked to the *kodomo-ya*, or child shops.

These days in Japan, at first glance, it would seem that gays have been able to maintain the spirit of liberation evident centuries ago. Blatantly homosexual entertainers are frequently honored guests on TV roundtable discussions. Tokyo's Shinjuku 2-chome quarter is home to many hundreds of establishments catering to gays—bars, bookstores, and love hotels. Despite the mass market, the life of an *o-kama* in Japan in the late twentieth century is not one that most are eager to display. For most gays, their true sexual identity remains a secret from friends, co-workers, family—even wives. Many Tokyo gay bars are packed with men wearing wedding rings. They are solid salarymen and doting fathers. A couple of nights a week or more, however, they quaff a few beers with their gay comrades and perhaps enjoy a gay sex show or a male tryst in a love hotel before heading home to the wife waiting with a late-night snack.

The gay *gaijin* in Japan is likely to find companionship as easy as his straight counterpart. The fear of AIDS has prompted many establishments in the gay quarters to bar foreigners, especially the sauna baths of conservative Ueno, but *gaijin* are still welcome in many of Shinjuku 2-chome's haunts. For the gay *gaijin* man in Japan looking to dive into the scene there is no better place to start than GB in Shinjuku 2-chome. It has a regular crowd of foreigners and Japanese who chat amiably with newcomers while checking out the videos. The bar owner prides himself on operating an establishment with an American atmosphere and is happy to begin chatting in English with a first-timer. GB used to make no secret about what kind of place it was, until a recent remodeling it displayed a "No Women Allowed" sign. Nowadays the giveaway is inside. Even on weekday nights GB is packed. Every patron is male and on some nights predominately foreign—ranging from young English teachers with British accents to veteran American journalists recounting war stories. GB has a reputation of being a meat market—some are just looking to meet old friends, others are looking to quickly make new ones of a more intimate variety. For those who get lucky at GB and can't wait to get to know each other better, the Love Star Hotel next door and other inns close by are happy to provide short-time accommodations to male couples.

But a fellow need not go to such effort and expense for a quickie. Around the corner, just across the street from the Shinjuku 3-chome subway station exit on Hanazono-dori is the high-rise BYGS (pron. "bigs") Shinjuku Building. Although the activity is not sanctioned by the building's owners, the toilet stalls in the evenings are a popular spot for men to meet and have a go with younger lads.

Another spot user-friendly for the gay newcomer to Tokyo is Fuji, just around the corner from Hotel T. It features videos on the wall, high-tech modern decor, English-speaking bartender, and an approximately fifty-fifty mix of *Nihonjin* and *gaijin*. Across the street from Fuji, on the second floor, is Lamppost. It also caters to a classy and well-mannered crowd who eschew the videos for a piano bar. On any night a few foreigners can be found gathered around its marble-topped tables and small counters.

Among the most comfortable and friendly spots in Shinjuku 2-chome is Kusu-O, which displays a sign outside with its name in kanji, meaning Kyushu Man. After stepping inside you get a feeling that you have just been transported to a 1980s-era San Francisco fern bar except that most of the customers are young Japanese men with closely cropped hair. Foreign gays who speak some Japanese are warmly welcomed.

In the gay world there are different strokes for different folks. Some are most comfortable in the short-hair bars, others are looking for something a bit more on the wild side. For the adventursome Sazai is the place. It attracts a weird mix of patrons, especially young men who go in for body piercing. It's a renowned late-night spot and probably not worth checking out before 2 a.m.

Another nocturnal favorite is Kinsmen which on weekend attracts not only gay men, but lesbians, bisexuals, and heterosexuals who desire a place to hang out with their gay friends. Everyone is quite friendly and Kinsmen is even brash enough to hire a female bartender! However this has been the only spot where, even accompanied by a gay *gaijin* friend, I had men overtly coming on to me. A European fellow sidling up to the bar to refresh his drink introduced himself by saying "You are very beautiful." I thanked him for the compliment and went back to the conversation with the guy I had walked in with. I wondered, if perhaps, he could tell that the two of us were not a couple. At the end of the night as my buddy and I were about to depart, an inebriated Japanese fellow made a beeline for me as I headed toward the door, suddenly laid a wet smacker on my lips and asked me in Japanese if I'd be so kind as to go with him to a love hotel. Snapping myself out of momentary disbelief, I gave him a smile, put my arm around my friend's shoulders, and told the amorous gent that I was already taken for the evening.

No visit to the neighborhood is complete without a stop at Books Rose. Foreign gays consider the shop a good place to browse and cruise, and it has the added benefit of staying open until three a.m. It also sells some very peculiar items including popper-like sniffers that some swear are chemically identical to amyl nitrate. Who said Japan had the strictest drug laws? The bookstore itself provides a good education in the peculiarities of gay life in Japan. Browsing through the magazines will quickly make it evident that there are different segments of the gay community in Tokyo. *Samson* is dedicated to readers who prefer their lovers to be tubby. *Adon* is for the young and healthy set. *Sabu*, with a cover proclaiming in English "Magazine For MEN Who Love MEN," caters to those who prefer athletic men of all ages. The photo sections of the magazines do not display penises and the comic strips also do not explicitly show sex organs although men in bondage or rape acts flourish. Sadly, the gay magazines seem to be filled with the violent fantasies that also flourish in the heterosexual magazines. *Samson*, *Adon*, and *Sabu*, however, do provide listings and advertisements featuring gay bars, health clubs, massage parlors, S&M shops, and video stores throughout Tokyo and other major cities in Japan. The ads also give an indication of the state of welcome for *gaijin*—a few ads include photos of handsome young foreign men but others read "Japanese Only" or "please foreigners rebrain (sic) from entering." Like the bars for straights in Tokyo it helps to have an introduction to enter many establishments. Many are hole in the wall joints, packed with men. The guys, Japanese and foreign, who are regulars at GB or Fuji are likely to be happy to introduce a novitiate to the more exclusive establishment of Shinjuku 2-chome.

A more low-key establishment that is a nice place to stop during any part of the evening is M&M, across from Books Rose, where one of the masters of this small bar is a Canadian. M&M, of course, rolls out the welcome mat for foreigners. Other more discrete establishments, such as Nawa, likely require an introduction. There are no lights on the main second floor of Nawa, only candles at the table. The bartender will place a colored coaster below patrons' drinks. He knows which color to put before the regulars—black for the sadists and red for the masochists. The first-timers and those who don't dally in S&M get a brown coaster. For a payment to the bar of a couple thousand yen or so, a pair can retire to the third floor and privately entertain themselves. But the most interesting things seem to take place on the second floor.

Enema shows are popular events these days in which a cute lad is given a colonic in front of an enthusiastic audience. This kind of bizarre ritual is obviously one that many foreign non-gays would like to see if only for the perverse thrill of writing a letter back home to tell the folks, "You wouldn't believe what I saw in a bar here the other night..." Well, a word of warning to the straights who have made it this far through this chapter, gays here frown on gawking straights on their turf. "The bartenders have a kind of radar and foreign straights are likely to be detected and evicted," says one gay Brit who is a regular in 2-chome. Straights who really want a look at the quarter should go only in the company of a gay friend, and as I found out, it can take some persuading to get them to take you into their world. If they do, you should feel that they consider you a trusted pal. Fellow straights, rest assured, although you may have to contend with a few good-natured rubs from bartenders and mama-sans, some of whom offer no hanky-panky shoulder massages on greeting their regulars, no one is likely to make an unsolicited grab for your privates. (The only time this has happened to me was in a Kabukicho hostess club when the gay male Taiwanese manager wanted to compare sizes.)

Even for the gay patrons of 2-chome one of the biggest fads in the area these last few years can be a bit unsettling the first time they experience it. It's *Fundoshi* Night—the Japanese gay bar version of the toga party where everyone is mandated to don the buttocks-revealing belts of sumo wrestlers! For many overseas gay visitors no trip to Japan can be complete without joining a roomful of Japanese gays strutting around like scantily clad sumo warriors.

For those who are looking for something even a bit more participatory 2-chome abounds with host clubs and gay S&M bars which offer a menu of services starting from ¥8000. At many clubs young men are available for short-time stays at the neighborhood love hotels. Prices vary as do enthusiasm for servicing foreigners.

Heterosexual foreigners, and gays too, who get their first look at Shinjuku 2-chome are likely to be amazed by the immensity of the quarter which seems to stretch for a number of city blocks in every direction and with multi-story buildings featuring gay bar over gay bar. On the streets, gay cruising is popular with drivers slowing to eye the boys hanging out on the street corners. On some weekends it causes traffic jams in the area. Yet, the police maintain only a discrete presence. The secret to all this can be discovered when the rare fight breaks out. The bartender will quickly pick up the phone and make a call. It is not the officers of the law who come running but members of the *yakuza*. Like the rest of the pink world the gay bars pay their protection money to the gangs and prefer to call on the *yakuza* to handle their dirty work rather than get the police involved. The gay world is tidy and shuns the headlines. The police sometimes do conduct raids rooting out some of the underaged boys working as male prostitutes or busting foreign hosts who have overstayed their visas. These are the few times the mainstream press pays attention to the gay world. The rest of the time its only visible presence is when the *o-kama* talents take to the airwaves.

Unlike in America and European countries Japan doesn't have marches for gay rights. Few outside the entertainment arena flaunt their homosexuality. Unfortunately for the gay community there are few people like 2-chome bar owner Ken Togo, an avowed homosexual, who has run in parliamentary elections. The straight electorate, however, has not seen fit to put into office Japan's first openly gay politician.

GIRLS ONLY:
LESBIAN HANGOUTS

▼▼▼▼▼▼▼▼▼▼▼▼▼▼▼▼▼▼▼▼▼▼▼▼▼▼▼▼

While there are many recorded examples in Japanese history exhorting the virtues of male-to-male sexual unions, the female version remains relatively unmentioned. There are stories of the shoguns' courtesans and Buddhist nuns resorting to lesbianism but the reason seems to be that these women embraced each other primarily because they did not receive adequate masculine attention rather than a true desire for another female body.

Only in the last decade or so have lesbians been able to enjoy each other's company in a few Tokyo bars dedicated to them. But in contrast to the hundreds of male-only bars in Shinjuku 2-chome alone the pubs catering exclusively to gay ladies are sparse. The most common meeting ground for girls who like girls is the semi-private disco party. Gay women usually have at least one night a month reserved for them at popular discos. The scene does not blatantly advertise its presence. The key is to read a bit between the lines. Deep disco, for example, calls its girls' night "Purple Pit." At

Gold, one of Tokyo's most in-spots for the early 90s, the lesbian disco night is dubbed "Mona Lisa."

Many gay women (as is the case with gay men in Japan) are married and doting parents. One aerobics studio in Shinjuku is frequently rented out by an informal lesbian group for parties. The wives and mothers can make an honest excuse that they will be spending the evening out with the girls trying to get their bodies into a little better shape. Hubbies don't seem to mind, none the wiser, when their women return home with smiles on their faces that the men haven't seen in weeks! But for the foreign woman in Tokyo not in the small and wary network there are places to go to expand her sexual horizon. Among the most friendly and affordable is Sunny, located in the Shinjuku 2-chome gay district. But Sunny is not strict about gender of clientele and it is not uncommon to see men in the place. Madonna and Mars are the two other lesbian bars that are relatively friendly to newcomers and *gaijin no onna* (foreign women) but they are a bit on the pricey side. For the woman who just doesn't want to look at another man (straight or gay) for the evening, the place to go is Mars which is very strict about not admitting men.

The few women I've met in Japan (foreign and native) who are willing to admit that they've been to these place say the lesbian scene in Tokyo is a tiny one and, unlike the gay male world here, you won't find hotels, sauna baths, and book stores catering to gay women. The only public displays of women getting it on together seem to be played out on the stages of the nude theaters where a pair of women act out the fantasy of *kai awase* (the joining of shellfish) for an audience that is exclusively heterosexual and male.

10

WALK ON THE WILD SIDE

S&M SCENE

▼▼▼▼▼▼▼▼▼▼▼▼▼▼▼▼▼▼▼▼▼▼▼▼▼▼▼▼▼

At first it appears to be just another run-of-the-mill strip routine as the young buxom woman, clad in black, sits down on a chair on the stage and begins to undress. As she sheds all of her garments, except for leather suspenders supported by her shoulders and thighs, the show begins to take on a more unusual aspect. The lady moves forward onto the stage and stands upon a mat. She lights three candles tied together and mesmerizes the audience for the next 15 minutes. As the candle begins to melt, the star of the show slowly rotates on the mat—making sure all sides of the audience get a peak at her ample breasts—and begins dripping the hot wax over her body. No part of her anatomy is spared—the wax drips onto her back, her large breasts, her ankles, and finally onto her vagina, not only singeing all of her pubic hairs but by the end of the show wilting them to a crisp. "Bet you've never seen anything like this back home," I say to my guest, an American movie producer who had been boasting about the "topless and even bottomless" strip joints he had been in back in the States. "No, you're right about that," he admits humbly as his eyes are transfixed by the large flame burning atop the trio of candles.

Japan's sexual arena abounds with the practices of sadism and masochism. It permeates the comic books, the porno films (now usually called AV—adult videos), and more and more these days, the live shows. Anyone who is just looking for a straightforward striptease is, by Tokyo standards, downright old-fashioned. Well, I guess I am a passé fogy of the nth degree because in the course of researching this book there was one experiment I could not bring myself to conduct—submitting to the strap of one of Tokyo's abundant S&M queens. Go ahead, call me old-fashioned, call me a coward, I'll admit it. Not that I wasn't just a little tempted, however. After all I had heard of the exploits of Tokyo's queen of queens—Tomoko Minami.

Tomoko rides herd at a club in Shibuya called Wild Cat. She has seen in her few short years as a mistress of the whip a one time fetish of, as she likes to put it, "a tiny group of maniacs," blossom into a popular pastime of ordinary Japanese folk. One appearance by Tomoko on a recent TV program prompted hundreds of phone calls to her club asking for directions and appointments. On a given day, Tomoko finds herself dishing out well-paid-for abuse at a rate of seven to 12 customers a day. What she does she apparently does very well because many, she claims, are repeat customers. But it's a new breed of pain seekers seeking the queens. "Most of the first-timers are lame. One crack of the whip on their behinds and they're crying out, '*itai! itai!*'" says one S&M club mama-san. Tomoko contends that some of her clients are quite famous, others are from the legions of salarymen and students we sit with everyday on the trains and subways. All in all, they range in age from teens to the eighties.

What's the average salaryman like facing a good paddling? The S&M queens say most are looking for a release from the mundane lives where they must play the role of a proper husband and good company employee. In the hands of a dominatrix they can be another self—some even yelp like a girl in a voice they have seen on screen from porn actresses in S&M movies. Most S&M queens pick up the torture instruments after a few years of handling men's cocks in the cabarets and soaplands. They say they prefer their present line of employment because they can have total control over their clients. "They don't want us to play passive roles, they want to be dominated," explains Saiko, who does exactly that at an Ikebukuro club.

A number of the S&M haunts say they've been seeing a lot of couples lately coming in for shared beatings. The wives usually make the call, explaining that they're looking to spice up their boring sex life or hoping to jolt their husbands out of impotence. It seems to work and the doting housewives seem to get something out of it too. "At first the wife is just watching her husband and me, but then she becomes excited and gets into the act too," says Saiko. Perhaps the family that whips together sticks together.

Whips and sticks, however, are not my cup of tea, but I knew that this chapter would not be made whole without a firsthand observation of what exactly goes on behind closed chamber doors. Thus I did what any enterprising author on deadline would do in such a fix. I asked the craziest pal I knew in Tokyo—a *gaijin* I may add—to be my stand-in. In order to protect his little remaining public integrity and his high-paying job with a prestigious multi-national firm he shall not be further identified. But I hand over my keyboard to him at this juncture and allow him to complete the picture.

Ahem, thanks very much Steven. I have to agree with your initial assessment that to the uninitiated, spending time with a mistress of dominance does not seem to smack of good fun. Your first impression (and fear) is that you know you're in for a hiding, you think it's going to hurt and you don't know the ropes.

With only one place of reference, a dive in Shinjuku's notorious Kabukicho, this tale must necessarily be told from the beginning. I quickly found out that being a *gaijin* is already one strike against you, as the S&M world Tokyo-style is a furtive place, virtually closed to non-Japanese, even those with a strong sempiternal bent. It requires persistence and a genuine respect for the seedy side of life to gain admittance to such a club. Mr. Clemens, not knowing anyone who would admit to be turned on by the smack of leather against their back, turned to a healthy heterosexual male who likes his beer and will do most anything for a laugh. Well, that's me. Agreeing to do it (a commitment made after a night full of brewskies) is one thing. The buildup is another. By the time the Big Night finally rolled around I found myself wondering how I'd gotten into it. (You talked yourself into it, Clemens reminds me.) He was right.

That said, we march down to Ikebukuro—one of the dirtiest areas in town—with numerous clips of S&M classifieds. We'd been told by previous calls to two of the establishments that being *gaijin* would be no prob-

lem. "Head down to the telephone booth by the bank and call us from there. We'll give you further directions," we were told in our penultimate phone call. I felt we were on the verge of crossing the cultural boundary, entering the world of taboo. Then something went wrong with our connection. Perhaps Steven's Japanese accent was a little bit too slick, perhaps it was a little bit too thick due to the generous helpings of beer we had consumed in order to steel ourselves for the encounter. *"Gaijin dame,"* comes the reply from the club we must only be a few meters from. The same reply comes from the second club we phone back. "But we'd been told it would be okay," Steven intones. There is no reversal of the verdict. Thinking God has given me a break and I will never have to find out about pain, my thoughts turned to home as the author hails a cab and barks *"Shinjuku, Kabukicho no mae."* Desperate, we approach a tout in Kabukicho and explain our mission. He escorts us off to a place that turns out to be a strip joint. "No thanks," we reply when we discover the true nature of the establishment. It is S&M or bust for us. And then, like a sign from the heavens (or in this case, the third floor) is a neon invitation beckoning us with the English letters "SM."

Three flights up the stairs of the dingy building, the mama-san drops any pretensions of exclusivity when Mr. Clemens unrolls a wad of bills. We are in! "Go to it," says the pleased author with a wicked smile. The menu lists three courses—hard, medium, and soft. We tell the mama-san we'd like the most we can get for our money—¥20,000. (Steven has to dole out another ¥15,000 to suffer through a 30-minute floor show in the adjoining room where he joins a tiny audience of salarymen watching a young fellow, known as Kappa, wearing only a tiny red sock over his shriveled prick, hoist himself halfway to the ceiling with a chain attached to his little member and proceed to burn himself with wax dripping from a candle.)

Now to the meat of my story. Mari-chan, my queen for the hour, orders me to strip in a mirrored alcove off the main stage area. Only a partially closed thin plastic divide separates us from the floor show. Paddles, whips, chains, and spike collars hang from a rack on the wall. Standing in my briefs, feeling like a dweeb, Mari barks me into the buff. I have great reservations about revealing what happens next but the anonymity guaranteed by the esteemed publishers emboldens me. In what is the most humiliating moment of my life Mari orders me into a pink G-string, slips a rubber on my knob, and proceeds to tie me up, arms behind my back. Miles, it seems, of hemp go around my neck, waist, over the shoulders and finally—I am not paying too much attention to detail—a knot around my nuts and, yank, she pulls the cord and closes it with a knot around my chest. A cruel smile crosses her lips as I yelp. Too late to pull out now, trussed up like a giant chicken. "So you enjoy your job?" I ask in Japanese with all the innocence of a john on his first foray with a pro. "I love it," she hisses before telling me to shut up. She grabs a paddle, big enough to use for canoeing down the Amazon. "You're not going to hit me with that?" I shriek, genuine alarm in my voice. "It's softer than the whips," she replies. And with that consolation she orders me onto my stomach with my bum in the air. Nothing could have prepared me for what happens next. A searing pain in my backside erupts as she rams a plastic penis-shaped vibrator up my arsehole with all the finesse of a longshoreman tying a ship to dock! She dallies with a whip, its many tassels flaying my goose-pimpled flesh. I protest. She lashes me harder. I laugh. She lashes me harder. There is nothing I can do, she has total control.

Mari-chan, a pert but dumpy 24-year-old, is wearing a black mini the size of a band-aid and black halter top, her breasts bursting out. I ask her for a fuck. "No way," she says. And with that she rolls me over and runs a mushroom-shaped vibrator across my dick. More lashings, but they no longer seem painful. "Harder?" she asks. "Nope, it's okay just like that," I reply. S&M or not, I am in a situation where I am naked and with a woman. The brain orders me to have an orgasm whatever the cost. "How about if I eat you," I ask hoping for something that seems, at this point, a tad more conventional. She slips out, comes back a moment later, lifts ¥10,000 from my wallet, slides out of her black panties and starts to lower herself onto my face. I show her a deep smile of appreciation. And then, she pisses in my face. After the shower ceases, she wipes me with a towel and nestles down. The animal act is over but one final indignity awaits. I had forgotten about that vibrator chugging away for nearly an hour. One second it's there, the next it's whipped out and I swear, I thought I had spilled my guts.

"So how was it?" asks the author as I enter the stage area, the unease of Japanese salarymen evident as a *gaijin* emerges in their ranks. "Funny thing is I loved it," I tell him as we emerge once again into the Shinjuku night.

As a postscript I (Clemens the chicken) must add that I found an opportunity to return to the scene of the above abode of sadism several weeks later. America-based comedienne Tamayo Otsuki, a wild and crazy woman on her first return trip to Japan in a decade, asked me to take her to the wildest place I knew. Since she had already been treated to a nude show in Nagoya by a concert promoter I figured I had to do one better. A live S&M show, I surmised, would surely transfix this jaded lady, a veteran of decadent Hollywood. I was right. The small audience was greeted by two performers I was previously acquainted with—dominatrix Mari-chan and her colleague Kappa. During their 45-minute performance Mari-chan humiliated poor Kappa, again clad only in a tiny red sock on the tip of his prick, whipping and burning him. The most amusing part of the show came when Kappa took a black marker and transformed his stomach and groin into the face of an elephant. "But if you are an elephant then you must have a long nose," said Mari in a severe voice. Mari hauled out a vacuum cleaner, one of those industrial types, attached the long nozzle around Kappa's cock and turned it on. It brought a smile to his face. Tamayo turned to me and said in an announcer's tone, "Do not try this at home, these are professionals." I replied in a sotto voice, "Don't worry I only use my household appliances for their intended purposes." The S&M performance climaxed, so to speak, with Mari pissing into a bowl and commanding Kappa to drink it. He complied and told us, "It's delicious." Neither of us had a witty comeback to that.

11

COUNTRY PLEASURES

THE COUNTRY CLUB

▼▼▼▼▼▼▼▼▼▼▼▼▼▼▼▼▼▼▼▼▼▼▼▼▼▼▼▼▼▼▼

Tokyo is a more than adequate base of operations for the type of man who engages in the sexual sport of country hunting. Some readers, especially feminists, are likely to be aghast when learning what is involved in this particular sport, although women are just as welcome to compete. However, as with the hunters who use guns to collect their heads, the sport of country hunting seems to attract many more males than females. The rules of country hunting are simple—to bed objects of your sexual desire by their nations of origin. Country collecting is a longtime pursuit of travelers, stamp collectors, and ham radio operators. Each country is worth a point but some nations are quite rare on the list and evidence of a catch from a particular country earns large egotistical points from fellow collectors if nothing else. Travelers can verify their count by visas stamped in passports. Philatelists have the evidence in their stamp albums and amateur radio buffs exchange QSL cards.

Those of the sexual variety can provide no such evidence as it is tough to ask for an affidavit stating country of origin shortly after a fleeting sexual liaison. This had led to a gentlemen's agreement, so to speak, among the players—never lie about a country you haven't earned. Believe it or not, while most fishermen will perhaps exaggerate the size of a good catch, most fellas in the country hunting fraternity do not dare tell a fib. The reason is simple—once a fraud is discovered (and it will happen eventually to the habitual) the liar is ostracized from the story-swapping table. This has happened in Tokyo during the past year to two respected expatriates, members of The Century Seekers' Club (Tokyo Yurakucho Lodge 417) who were revealed to have tried to credit garden-variety Thais as rare Nepalese. Shame on them.

Among straight men, there are three types of country hunters. There are those who collect girls by nation solely based on legitimate pickups, meaning no money exchanges hands or other body parts. Another division collects its countries by buying them—i.e. sleeping with hookers from foreign countries at home and seeking them out abroad. The third category is composed of those who don't give a hoot how they bed their women. To be frank I've done much better at country collecting with stamps and on shortwave radio but I've picked up enough to acquire a healthy interest in the game. My friend, Sammy, however is among the world-class players.

Sammy agreed to meet me one night in Shinjuku for an interview. I was eager to hear what such a master would say. As we spooned down our dishes of *bibimbap* in a Korean restaurant on the fringe of Kabukicho Sammy confided that he wasn't sure just how many nationalities he had bedded. "The first 35 I can recite off the top of my head but after that it gets kinda fuzzy," he said. "The problem is of classification." "What do you mean, 'classification?'" I asked. "What I mean is this—say you pick up this hooker in Moscow next week. She speaks fluent Russian and has lived in Moscow for ten years but the government, on her passport, considers her home to be in Belarus where she lived before coming to the Soviet capital. Her mother is from Kazahkstan and her father was a half-Austrian Jew born in Germany—East Germany." "Ah, the geopolitic thing has a way of making it fuzzy," I said sipping on my Korean *shōchū*. "Precisely. She was a Soviet citizen. But is she now a Russian or a Belarus-whatever-they-call-it-now-ian? Besides that, she's half Kazakh or something and half former East German maybe." Sammy looked truly perplexed and agitated by the scenario he had raised. "I think you'd need a specialty in international law to figure these things out," I said, trying to console him. "Yeh, I guess you're right."

Trying to change the direction of the conversation I asked, "So what's the toughest country to bag?" Sammy laughs. "Take a guess." "Hmm," I said trying to conjure up an image of a world map in my *shōchū*-rattled brain. "I'd imagine some off the beaten path, very conservative country where they cut off your pecker for touching a woman you're not married to. I'd say Yemen or Oman." "Not a bad guess and these things being subjective you might have a contender in Oman. But Yemen is not a difficult one at all. There are plenty of Yemenites running around Israel and some of them are pros. And, of course, you don't have to score in their country of origin so Yemen is definitely not a top ten rarity." "So what's the one you'd really like to rack up and have not been able to get?" He leaned over the table with a very serious expression on his face, picked up his glass, took a sip, and looked me straight in the eye. "The Democratic People's Republic of Korea," he said. Sammy didn't know of any hostess clubs in Tokyo with North Korean women but he knew of one spot down the road where the nationalities were varied. "One month they were mostly Taiwanese, Thais, and Singaporeans. But there's been a turnover recently I've heard," he said as we walked to a spot called Club Michiko.

We were welcomed graciously at Michiko. It turns out that Sammy is a regular and on good terms with one of the Shanghai girls who works there. As Sammy flattered the ladies with his fluency in Cantonese, Mandarin, Taiwanese, and Fukien dialects of Chinese I struck up a conversation with the mama-san, Kaori. We knew the rules before stepping in—¥10,000 for all we could drink, ¥30,000 for a short-time take out and ¥40,000 for an all-nighter—so Kaori and I discussed the other side of business. "Yes, the end of the bubble economy is really hurting all the clubs around here," she said. I then asked her if it was true that some of the clubs had consolidated as a result, sharing their hostesses and shuttling them from one to another depending on where the clients were flowing at a particular hour. "It's nothing formal but some of the girls do go from club to club. If there's something in particular you're looking for just let me know and we can likely deliver," the Tokyo native said with the confidence of an Osaka mama-san. "Thanks, I'll keep that in mind," I replied.

Sammy and I had been sandwiched between a couple of young lovelies who turned out both to be from—surprise—Myanmar, otherwise known as Burma. When this was announced I saw Sammy's eyes light up. "I've never had a Burmese," he said with glee. Sammy obviously hadn't been making the round lately with much thoroughness. I had discovered that the influx of Burmese had begun about six months previous and had traced them to the *yakuza's* Thai connection. The girls were crossing the border in northern Thailand—filtering into towns like Chiang Mai and Chiang Rai where they could easily meet *Japayuki* brokers. A passport of either Burmese or Thai origination would be supplied and soon they were on their way to Narita where they would ease their way through the immigration process.

Ever since the government of the Philippines had begun yelping about the rough (read that sometimes fatal) treatment Filipinas were receiving in the *mizushōbai* world in Japan, the *yakuza* decided to recruit women from another poor Asian country where the government was likely to be preoccupied by other things more pressing to its survival than treatment of *Japayuki*. Burma was a natural. The Burmese mix in easily with their Thai sisters since most, by the time they make it to the hostess bars of Japan, have picked up enough Thai language ability to take orders from their Bangkok-born mamasans.

Sammy headed out with his date, prompting me to pay up my ¥10,000 tab for the cheap Nikka whisky I had guzzled and the Burmese I had ogled. Not long after I found myself chatting with the multilingual Kabukicho street tout who calls himself Tommy. Tommy has always been evasive about his true nationality—being that he speaks fluent Chinese, Korean, and Japanese (with an Okinawa dialect) you can take your own guess. Tommy tries to steer me toward Club Nikol. I recite an abbreviated version of the aforementioned saga from the esteemed Nikol. At the conclusion, Tommy promises to try to recover the outstanding diamond earring, saving a visit and ¥10,000. Tommy has no idea I'm researching a book and just considers me one of the well-heeled horny *gaijin* about Kabukicho. He promises to try to get me into a club which doesn't have a habit of opening the door for *gaijin*.

Being a bit low on the cash flow I flash my American Express Gold yen card at the door which seems to ease the concern of the owner a tad. He gives me a verbal test drive in colloquial Japanese and passing that exam asks if I have a *gaijin tōrokusho*—identity card. I assure him that I do and am relieved that I don't have to produce it because it includes my mass media identity.

Seated on the sofa inside the spacious and plush Club Chant Larra I am quickly entranced by a very engaging 31-year-old Thai mama-san who formally introduces me to my quiz master, Mr. A, the club's affable owner who is a respected interior designer. After a few *karaoke* songs and more tumblers of second-rate whiskey I find myself commiting the worst mistake a first timer can make in this kind of establishment—I'm falling head over heels for the mama-san and making no secret of it. Mr. A is sympathetic but makes it clear that mama (who goes by the Japanese name of Sayuri) is off limits. I remind myself that one has to be careful about these kind of entrées since it is not infrequent to discover there is more than just a business connection between owners and mamas. Sayuri is taking my flattery in the best of spirits, knowing that between the amount of spirits in my system and the dim lighting, I have projected her as a divine princess of lust, if not love.

Mama, upon hearing my recital of the exploits of my

friend Sammy and figuring I must have a pecadillish interest in the subject emits a smile that only deepens my desire for her. "I want to introduce you to a pair of young ladies you will find most interesting," she says. She escorts to my sofa seat two stunning young ladies. Sayuri is beaming as if she is introducing a couplet of rare Himalayan kittens to a feline fanatic. "I'm sure you'll be happy to know that they are both from Laos," mama-san announces. "Yes I am," I respond. This is where I found out that Sammy is a breed of country hunter superior to myself. I had no excuse nor moral reserve for not escorting either of these Laotian lovelies to the love hotel of their choice. But the truth be told, I discovered I am not an accountant of sex. Another number in the ledger could not dissuade me. If I could not be alone with over-30 mama-san from run-of-the-mill Thailand, I was not in the mood for love. A true member of the country club must be more calculating.

THE LAST WORD

▼▼▼▼▼▼▼▼▼▼▼▼▼▼▼▼▼▼▼▼▼▼▼▼▼▼▼▼▼▼▼

During the 18 months of exploration that led up to this final chapter I discovered that one of the primary characteristics of the *mizushōbai* is just how organic it is. Pink may be the primary color but the shades seem to change more frequently than the seasons. Prices and fads reflect the economic times. For every high-class, high-priced Ginza hostess bar that shut down, another seedy joint opened in some other less well-heeled part of town.

Not only does the pink world of Japan reflect the nation's economic fortunes but perhaps reveals something about its sociological standing as well. It would be interesting for an author of a more academic bent to explore this topic and attempt to explain why, for example, in the late 1980s a number of hands-on all-nude bars appeared where customers could fondle women to their hearts' content—with the women draped from neck to ankles in transparent tape. And why many of those establishments have now been transformed into S&M bars where customers pay extra to be urinated on while their office colleagues look on. What does that say about the current generation? Unfortunately the few places that sprouted up recently around Tokyo featuring topless female sumo wrestling have already cleared out their less than sacred *dohyō* to feature other kinds of shtick which are less tied to revered Japanese traditions. (One example is clubs featuring simultaneous masturbation with the male customer and hostess linked only by two-way video circuits.)

I've refrained, for other reasons, from listing the prolific tele-talk clubs where a fellow pays an hourly fee to sit in a room before a telephone and attempts to make a date with a mysterious lady calling in. A few of the incoming calls are from shills who, for a fee, will agree to meet the nervous male voice on the other end of the line for a sexual liaison, but most are unattractive young women or bored housewives looking for a brief telephonic thrill and usually don't show up for the promised encounter. Pachinko seems to offer about the same odds of scoring. The telephone clubs have permeated nearly every entertainment district of the Kanto district (and there seem to be as many of them as there are pachinko parlors). The foreign fellow whose Japanese is fluent enough to tackle this kind of diversion has likely already discovered before reading this book that trying to pick up women at random in coffee shops in Kichijoji will generate better odds of success. Cruising the streets, besides, is a heck of a lot cheaper and you can choose your women by their physical appearance rather than hoping to seduce a giggling voice on the other end of a cold plastic telephone receiver. I'm sure there are a few demented fellows out there who might find the phone thing appealing, even exciting. Well, that's why Tokyo's got a kink for every kinky guy or gal.

A few other parting notes of warning. A come-on from a haggard-looking middle-aged hooker outside the normal boundaries of street walkers (hint: there's no other women in high heels on the block) is likely to spell trouble. In all likelihood, the she is a he. The Koma Theatre area of Kabukicho, the back streets of Roppongi, and most of Yokohama are such infamous prowling spots for these types. Again, I know, there are some who go for this sort of thing. If so, I hope I have just given you some good leads.

Others may be disappointed to learn that the fad featuring naked women on stage fornicating with large dogs seems to have had its last bark, at least in the Tokyo area. Sex acts between non-Japanese Asian women and inebriated salarymen still take place. Again, try the back streets of Yokohama's numerous sleazy entertainment districts where they have no qualms about letting foreign men (including illegal day workers) join in on the action. Ray Ventura gives a detailed description of this type of activity in Chapter 12 of his unique book, *Underground in Japan*, which also intimately reveals the daily lives of some of the real down and out Southeast Asian women who sell their bodies in the squalid back alleys of Yokohama's Kotobuki district.

While I'm turning into a book reviewer in these last pages I should point out that there are a few other works out there which cover the subject of sex in Japan in a more comprehensive manner. Nick Bornoff's recent tome, *Pink Samurai*, approaches encyclopedic and manages to wax eloquently about the social significance of soaplands and other licentious establishments without ever providing the precise locations where the author had all his fun. Shame on you Nicholas for not sharing the only part of your notes we were really interested in seeing!

Mr. and Mrs. Longstreet, in their book *Yoshiwara: The Pleasure Quarters of Old Tokyo*, did a fine job detailing the old legal red-light district of Tokyo, giving us an idea of what was sadly extinguished by the authorities a few decades ago. There are a few cinders still smoldering out in that part of town around Asakusa and Ueno but it is difficult to find those establishments which are both barely hospitable and willing to cater to foreigners.

Another pair of Yen books—*Bachelor's Japan* and *Lover's Guide to Japan*—remain steady sellers and have, for decades, provided the newly arrived foreign male with a guiding light to the night life. Alas, author Boye de Mente (disputedly the most prolific *gaijin* author of all types of books on Japan) has semi-retired to beautiful Arizona and seems no longer to have the enthusiasm or the energy to update his fine pocket-sized books on his frequent forays back to Japan. It's an indicator of how much the times have changed to remember that *Bachelor's Japan* (mild in language and details) caused a considerable sensation in the Japanese media when it was first published.

I highly recommend *Making Out in Japanese*, and its sequel, written by the young Geers couple (an American lad and his Japanese bride) which should serve as companions to this book for anyone desiring to string together this book's glossary into coherent and pro-vocative sentences.

"Why did you want to write this book?" is a question I frequently heard from colleagues and friends when they learnt about my undertaking. Sometimes the question is asked with disgust, other times with sincere curiosity. Perhaps I see myself like the protagonist of Paul Theroux's book, *Saint Jack*, a part-time pimp who viewed his side work as a calling to save "many fellers from harm and many girls from brutes." The point here is that with or without encouragement or warnings from me or anyone else, a lot of foreign men are going to go on the prowl in Tokyo and there are going to be men and women out there trying to snare them. Hopefully this book will steer the fellows in the right direction, give them tips on how to make best first impression (very important in Japan) and what they can and cannot fondle for their hard-earned yen. If you agree with my intentions, tell a friend about this book—I need the royalties to recoup the expenditures for the extensive field research!

MAPS

YOSHIWARA

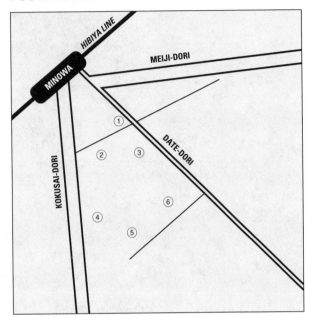

1 New Mika (soapland) **¥¥** *
2 Sukeroku (soapland) **¥¥**
3 Mink (soapland) **¥¥¥**
4 Crystal Lounge (soapland) **¥¥¥¥**
5 Bell Commons (soapland) **¥¥¥**
6 Chisa-na Koibito (soapland) **¥¥**

> * **¥** signifies a charge of ¥10,000 or less, **¥¥** ¥ 20,000 or less, etc.

SHINJUKU 2-CHOME

1 Kusuo (gay bar) ¥

2 M&M (gay bar) ¥

3 Kinsmen (gay/straight bar) ¥

4 Lamppost (gay bar) ¥

5 Fuji (gay bar) ¥

6 Ken (opera music gay bar) ¥

7 GB (*gaijin* gay bar) ¥

8 Johny Shonen (gay massage) ¥¥

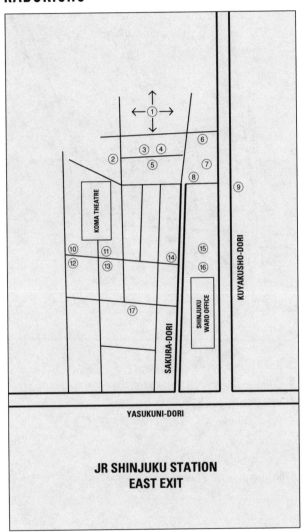

1 Streetwalkers ¥¥¥

2 Hinomaru (cabaret) ¥¥

3 Bell (take-out hostess) ¥¥¥

4 Ai (host bar) ¥¥

5 DX (nude theatre) ¥

6 New Ai (host bar) ¥¥

7 Club Michiko (take-out hostess) ¥¥¥

8 Chant Larra (take-out hostess) ¥¥¥

9 Club Nikol (take-out hostess) ¥¥¥

10 Mini Tokku (pink salon) ¥¥

11 Silk Heart (soapland) ¥¥¥¥

12 Pretty (lingerie pub) ¥¥

13 Bishonen (sex salon) ¥¥

14 TS (nude theatre) ¥

15 Pub Diamond (take-out hostess) ¥¥¥

16 New Art (nude theatre) ¥

17 Aphrodite (S&M) ¥¥¥ / ¥¥¥¥

ROPPONGI

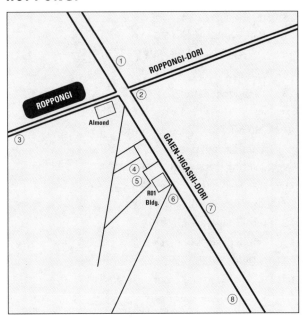

1 La Prestige (hostess bar) ¥¥
2 Touts and Pimps
3 BMW (fashion massage) ¥¥
4 Tropic of Cancer (hostess bar) ¥¥
5 Hard Rock Cafe (singles' bar) ¥
6 Krystal Roppongi (fashion massage) ¥¥
7 Club Casanova (hostess bar) ¥¥
8 Club ABC (S&M) ¥¥¥¥

OMIYA

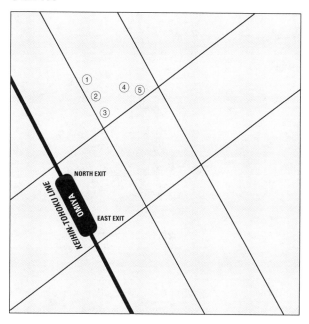

1 Kangofu "nurses" (soapland) ¥¥
2 Momoyama (soapland) ¥
3 Silvia (soapland) ¥
4 Otome (soapland) ¥
5 Mikado (soapland) ¥

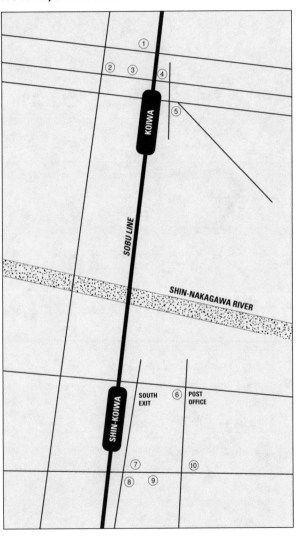

① ② ③ ④ ⑤

KOIWA

SOBU LINE

SHIN-NAKAGAWA RIVER

SHIN-KOIWA

SOUTH EXIT

⑥ POST OFFICE

⑦ ⑧ ⑨ ⑩

1 Top Cats (lingerie pub) ¥
2 Playboy (pink salon) ¥
3 NonNon (pink salon) ¥
4 Banana House (fashion massage) ¥/¥¥
5 Hana Monogatari (pink salon) ¥
6 Musical (cabaret) ¥
7 Idol (cabaret) ¥
8 Five Star (pink salon) ¥
9 Eve (pink salon) ¥¥
10 Kobuta no Yakata (pink salon) ¥

KINSHICHO

1 Yushima Steambath (soapland) ¥¥
2 Matsushima Steambath (soapland) ¥¥
3 LaForet (cabaret) ¥

PINK GLOSSARY

JAPANESE–ENGLISH

▼▼▼▼▼▼▼▼▼▼▼▼▼▼▼▼▼▼▼▼▼▼▼▼▼▼

ahō: fool
ai: love (n.)
aijin: lover
aijin banku: sexual date club (lit. lovers bank)
ainame: lesbian cunnilingus
ai shiteru: I love you
aitai: want to meet
akagai: cunt (lit. red clam)
akashi senkō: overnight fee to sleep with geisha
ana: hole
ana de yaritai: want to do it up the ass
anaru sekkusu: anal sex
asoko: sex organs (lit. over there)
AV: adult video
AV garu: porn actress

baidoku kensa: VD exam
bājin: virgin
bairin gyaru: bilingual girl
baishun: prostitution (lit. selling spring)
baka: foolish, stupid

bakkushan: seeing a nice ass
basuto: bust
beddo: bed
bideo bokkusu: porn video booth (lit. video box)
bishōnen: beautiful boy
bitamin esu: sperm (from vitamin S)
bobo: pussy
bodicon gyaru: young woman wearing tight-fitting clothes
bōifurendo: boyfriend
bokki: erection
busui gyaru: ugly girl

chausu: female on top
chibiri manko: dripping pussy
chibusa: breasts
chichi: tits
chīfu: club manager (lit. chief)
chikan: molester
chikubi: nipples
chimpo: cock, dick
chin chin: penis
chiro: slow comer (masc.)
chitsu: vagina
chō-mini panchira: micro-miniskirt revealing panties
chongā: bachelor

daburu sābisu: double service (some 69 variation)
daisuki: really like
dame: wrong, not allowed
dankon: cock (lit. male root)
danna-san: husband
dare demo: anyone
daruma geisha: (see korobi geisha)

dashita: ejaculated
debu: fatty
dembu: butt (polite)
dendo kokeshi: vibrator
desō: I'm coming (masc.)
dōhan: customer quota system for hostesses
doko demo: anywhere
dōtei: male virgin

eizu: AIDS
emu: cock; masturbation; masochist (from letter M)
emuteki: masochistic; butch
enchō: additional charge for extended time
erabitai: want to choose
ero (short for erochikku): erotic; porno
eroi: obscene
ero kanchō: erotic enema
esu: from letter S for sex, sperm, sadism, etc.
esu garu: sadistic girl; lesbian (from English sister)
etchi: from English letter h for hentai, perverted

fakku shitai: want to fuck
fasshon herusu: massage parlor (from English fashion)
fera: fellatio
fera no sābisu: fellatio service
fingā sābisu: finger service
funō: impotent
furūto: flute (see shakuhachi)

gandaka: huge dick (crude)
gārufurendo: girlfriend
gei: the arts (eumphemism for night world);
    can also mean gay
gei bā: gay bar

gei no sekai: art world (see mizushobai)
gōbō: a long dick
gohi-iki: geisha's regular client
gomasuri: flattery
gomora: lesbian (crude, from English Gomorrah)
gomu: rubber (from English gum)
gōruden shawa: golden shower
guramā: big breasted girl

hadaka: naked
hādo fera: strong blow job
haiban rōzeki: wild drinking party
hakebune: erect cock (lit. sail boat)
hako: pussy (lit. box)
hamaguri dekiru: can move vagina muscles
    (lit. can do the clam)
hamekonde: ram it in
hamete: put it in
hāmonika: cunnilingus (lit. harmonica)
hamoru: simultaneous orgasm
hanabira kaiten: club where girls rotate among
    customers
harigata: dildo
hatsukoi: first love
haya-uchi: to ejaculate quickly
hayaku: hurry up
henna gaijin: strange foreigner
herusu: (contraction of "health" massage)
heyadai: room rate
himo: pimp (lit. string)
himopan gyaru: hostess wearing string panties
hiningu: contraception
hosutesu ryō: hostess fee

ichigensan okotowari: members' only
ijirimakuri: fingering
iku iku: I'm coming!
immo: pubic hair
inkaku: clitoris (clinical)
inkei: penis (clinical)
inno: scrotum (clinical)
inpo: impotent
ippatsu: to come (climax) once
iroke nuki de nomu: drinking without girls
iroppoi: horny; sexy
iyarashii: nasty

japayuki: women from other Asian countries
    hostessesing in Japan
jikan desu: time's up
jirashiya: prick tease
jōji: love affair
jorō: slut
jun-nama: without condom (see nama)

kai-awase: pussy to pussy (lit. matching shells)
kamu auto: out of the closet
kanchō purē shitai: want to have an enema
kataku natteiru: it (penis) is becoming hard
kawaii: cute
ke: (pubic) hair
kechi: stingy
kechimbo: cheapskate
kekkon shita: got married
ketsu: ass
ketsu no ana: asshole
kichigai: crazy, nuts
kikuza: ass (lit. chrysanthemum)

kimochi: feeling

kinchaku: movement of vaginal muscles (lit. moving purse strings)

kintama: testicles (lit. golden balls)

kirai: hate

kirei: pretty

kissa(ten): coffee shop

kisu māku: hickey (lit. from English kiss mark)

kōgan: testicles (clinical)

koibito: lover

koibumi: love letter

koiwazurai: lovesick

kokachin: stiff dick

kokku sakkingu: cock sucking

kondōmu: condom

konyoku-buro: mixed bathing

korobi geisha: easy to be geisha (lit. rollover geisha)

kowai: afraid

kuchi no sābisu: blow job (lit. mouth service)

kudoku: make a pass

kurabu: club

kuraimakkusu: climax

kuri-chan: clitoris

kyabarē: blow job or hand job joint (from English cabaret)

kyaku: (usually o-kyakusan) customer

kyandē: fellatio (derived from English candy)

mada: not yet

maki maki: transsexual

makura jibiki: pillow dictionary

manējā: pimp (lit. manager)

manko (usually o-manko): pussy

mantoru: massage parlor located in residential bldg.

manzuri: masturbation (fem., lit. 10,000 strokes)
mara: dick
massāji: massage
masutābēshon (sometimes sutabeshon): masturbation
mata: crotch
mawashi: gang bang
mazui: terrible
mekake: mistress
mizushōbai: the night life world (lit. water trade)
mongen: curfew
mō-sugu: soon
munage: chest hair
mune: tits
musuko: dick (lit. son)

nakani shitai: want to come (orgasm) inside
naku: to come (lit. to cry)
nama: without condom (lit. raw)
namaiki: smart ass
namete kudasai: lick me please
neko yaru: gay sex (lit. to do cat)
netai: want to sleep
nezake: nightcap drink
nigiribobo: fist fucking (to female)
nikumanjū: cunt (lit. meat-filled bun)
nikutaiteki: voluptuous
ninshin shitakunai: don't want to become pregnant
nitōryū: bisexual (see ryotozukai)
nomitai: want to drink
nomitakunai: don't want to drink
nō-pan kissa: bottomless coffee shop
nozoki: peep show
nūdo gekijo: nude theatre
nugu jikan: time to take it off

nuide kudasai: please take it off
nureman: wet pussy

odoritai: want to dance
o-hanadai: time fee for hostess (lit. flower money)
o-inari-san: balls (crude)
o-jō-sama: queen (S&M)
o-kama: gay male, fag
o-koge: fag hag
o-nabe: lesbian
oku-san: wife
OL-taipu: office-lady type
o-manko-suri: vaginal masturbation
o-nabe: dyke
onanī: masturbation
one-san: sister (gay slang)
onna-no-ko: girl(s)
onsen geisha: hot springs geisha (usu. "loose" geisha)
oppai: breasts
orugasumu (sometimes pron. ogasamu): orgasm
osupe sābisu: hand-job service
otachi: bull dyke
otemba: tomboy
otoko-no-ko: boy(s)
owatta: finished
paiotsu: tits (crude Cockney-type slang)
paizuri: inserting penis between breasts
panpan garu: lady of the evening (slightly archaic)
pansuke: whore
pechapai: flat breasted
penisu: penis
pichi pichi: very small
pin!: schwing!
pinku: sexual (lit. pink)

pinpin-chan: cute stiff pecker
pitchi pitchi gyaru: fresh, lively girl

rabu hoteru: love hotel
rakon: circumcised dick
rankō: orgy
rennai kekkon: love marriage
rezubian (or rezu): lesbian
roman poruno: soft-porn movie
rorikon: lit. Lolita complex
rōshon massāji: lotion massage
ryōtōzukai: bisexual male (lit. using both swords)

sakaba: ordinary Japanese-style drinking bar
saku: condom; to suck (from English sock and suck)
saneko: clit
sanpi: ménage à trois
sarabobo: virgin-like pussy (crude)
sawannai: don't touch
sawaritai: want to touch
seibyō: venereal disease
seikō: sexual intercourse
seiyoku: sexual desire
sekkusu: sex
sekuhara bā: sexual harrasment bar
senzuri: masturbation (masc., lit. 1,000 strokes)
shakuhachi: fellatio (lit. bamboo flute)
shasei sangyō: ejaculation industry
shigoki: masturbation
shigoku shitai: want to stroke
shikijō: sexual passion
shikko: pee (n.)
shiko shiko suru: jerking off (v.)
shikkusu nain: 69

shimeiryō: fee to sit with specific hostess
shiri: (usually o-shiri), butt
shisutā bōi: effeminate man (lit. sister boy)
shōfu: prostitute
shojo: virgin
shomben: to piss (masc.)
shomben sābisu: golden shower
shujin: husband
sopurando: heterosexual bath house
soro: premature ejaculation
soso: pussy (crude)
suitchi: clit (from English switch)
sukebe: horny
sukebe jijii: dirty old man
suki desu ka: do you like it?
sumara yaritai: want to do it without a rubber (crude)
supā-daburu ekusutora sābisu: super-double
    extra service
supesharu sābisu: special service
surippu: fellatio with condom on
sutamina: (male sexual) stamina
sutanbai: girls on call (lit. standby)
suteki: wonderful
sutorippā: stripper
sutorippu gekijō: striptease theatre

tachiyaku: masculine gay
tanima no shirayuri: sperm between the breasts
    (lit. lilly in the valley)
tanoshikatta: was enjoyable
tanshō: small dick
temeko: vaginal masturbation
tento: hard-on (from English tent)
tomodachi ni naritai: want to be friends

toppuresu: topless
toruko: Turkish bath (now usually called sopurando)
tsubame: gigolo
tsumannai: boring

uiri shichatta: got a boner
ukemi: (gay) receiver
unko purē: shit play
ura omote: bisexual (or one who goes either way in gay sex)
uso da: it's a lie (freq. used kiddingly)
utsukushii: beautiful
uwaki: extramarital sex

wakai: young
wakai-ko: young girl(s)
wan wan: doggie style (sound of dog barking)
warui koto: a bad thing

yabai: dangerous
yakimochi: jealous
yami no onna: streetwalker
yarashii: lewd, filthy
yariman: slut
yaritai: want to do it
yasashii: kind, gentle
yopparai: drunk
yubizeme: finger fuck
yūjo: prostitute
yukkuri: slowly
yuna: public bath prostitute

zakone shitai: want to have group sex

ENGLISH-JAPANESE

▼▼▼▼▼▼▼▼▼▼▼▼▼▼▼▼▼▼▼▼▼▼▼▼▼▼▼

adult video: AV
afraid: kowai
AIDS: eizu
anal sex: anaru sekkusu
anyone: dare demo
anywhere: doko demo
ass: ketsu; kikuza (lit. chrysanthemum)
asshole: ketsu no ana

bachelor: chongā
bad: warui
balls: kintama; o-inari-san
bath: o-furo
bathhouse prostitute: yuna
beautiful: utsukushii; kirei; bijin
bed: beddo
big-breasted girl: guramā (lit. glamour)
big dick: gandaka; gōbō; kyokon; dekamara
bilingual girl: bairin gyaru
bisexual: nitōryu; ryōtōzukai (masc.); ura omote
blow job: fera; shakuhachi; kuchi no sābisu

blow-job joint: kyabarē (from English "cabaret"); pinsaro
boner: uiri (lit. wheelie)
boring: tsumannai
bottomless: nō-pan
boyfriend: bōifurendo
breasts: chibusa; oppai
bull dyke: otachi
bust: basuto
butch: emuteki
butt: dembu; o-shiri

catcher (gay): ukemi
chest hair: munage
circumcised: rakon
climax: kuraimakkusu
climax once: ippatsu
clitoris: inkaku; kuri-chan; saneko; suichi
cock: chimpo; dankon
comes quickly: haya-uchi (masc.)
come together: hamoru
coming: deso (masc.); iku
condom: kondōmu; gomu; sakku
contraception: hiningu
crazy: kichigai
crotch: mata
cunnilingus: hamonika; ainame (lesbian style)
cunt: nikumanju (lit. meat-filled bun)
curfew: mongen
customer: kyaku
cute: kawaii

dance: odoru
dangerous: abunai; yabai
dating club: aijin banku

dick: musuko
dildo: harigata
dirty old man: sukebe jijii
doggie style: wan wan (sound of dogs barking)
drunk: yopparai

effeminate man: shisutā bōi (lit. sister boy)
ejaculated: dashita
ejaculation industry: shasei sangyō
erect cock: kokachin
erection: bokki; hakebune
erotic: ero
erotic enema: ero kanchō
extramarital sex: uwaki

fag: o-kama
fatty: debu
feeling: kimochi
fellatio: fera; shakuhachi; furūto; kokku-sakkingu;
  kyandē
female on top: chausu
fingering: ijirimakuri; yubizeme
fist fucking: nigiribobo (to female)
flat breasted: pechapai
flattery: gomasuri
fool: baka; ahō
forbidden: dame
foreign hostess/prostitute: japayuki
friend: tomodachi

gang bang: mawashi
gay bar: gei bā
gay sex: neko yaru
geisha overnight fee: akashi senkō

gentle: yasashii
gigolo: tsubame
girlfriend: garufurendo
golden shower: gōruden shawā; shomben sābisu
group sex: zakone

hand job: osupe
hard-on: tento (from English tent)
hate: kirai
hooker: yūjo
horny: iroppoi; sukebe
hostess fee: hosutesu ryō; o-hanadai
hot-springs geisha: onsen geisha
husband: danna-san (someone else's); shujin

impotent: funo; inpo

jealous: yakimochi
jerk off: skiko shiko

lesbian: rezu; esu gyaru; gomora
lesbian sex: kai-awase (lit. matching shells)
lewd: yarashii
lie: uso
like: suki
Lolita complex: rorikon
lotion massage: rōshon massāji
love: ai
love affair: jōji
love hotel: rabu hoteru
love letter: koibumi
love marriage: rennai kekkon
lover: koibito; aijin
lovesick: koiwazurai

marriage: kekkon
masculine gay: tachiyaku
masochist: mazo; emuteki
massage: herusu (from "health massage")
massage parlor: fasshon herusu
masturbation: masutābēshon; senzuri (masc.); manzuri (fem.); shigoki
members' only: ichigensan okotowari (lit. no first-timers)
ménage à trois: sanpī
mistress: mekake
mixed bathing: konyoku buro

naked: hadaka
nasty: iyarashii
nightcap: nezake
nipples: chichi; chikubi
nude: nūdo
nude show: nūdo gekijo

obscene: eroi
orgasm: orugasumu; ōgasamu
orgy: rankō
overtime charge: enchō

pee: shikko
peep show: nozoki
penis: inkei; penisu
perverted: etchi (used kiddingly in hostess bars); hentai
pimp: himo; manējā
pitcher-catcher (gay): ura omote
porn actress: AV gyaru
porn booth: bideo bokkusu (lit. video box)
premature ejaculation: sōrō
pretty: kirei

prick tease: jirashiya
privates: asoko (lit. over there)
prostitute: shōfu
prostitution: baishun (lit. selling spring)
pubic hair: immo; ke
pussy: o-manko; bobo; hako (lit. box); soso

receiver (gay): ukemi
room rate: heyadai
rubber: gomu (lit. gum)

scrotum: innō
service: sābisu
sex: sekkusu
sexual: pinku
sexual desire: seiyoku
sexual harrassment: sekuhara
sexual intercouse: seikō
sexual passion: shikijō
sexual stamina: sutamina (masc.)
shit: unko
sixty-nine: shikkusu-nain (lit. six nine)
slowly: yukkuri
slut: jōro; yariman
small dick: tanshō
snapping pussy: kinchaku; hiku hiku bobo
soapland: sōpurando
sperm: bitamin esu (lit. vitamin S); zamen; seishi
stingy: kechi; kechimbo
streetwalker: yami no onna; panpan gyaru
stripper: sutorippā
striptease theatre: sutorippu gekijō

terrible: mazui

testicles: kintama; kogan
time limit: jikan seigen
tits: chikubi; chichi; mune; paiotsu
tomboy: otemba
topless: toppuresu
transsexual: maki maki
Turkish bath: toruko (now called soapland)

ugly girl: busui gyaru

vagina: chitsu
vaginal masturbation: o-manko suri; temeko
venereal disease: seibyō
VD exam: baidoku kensa
vibrator: dendō kokeshi
virgin: bājin; shojo; dōtei (male)
voluptuous: nikutaiteki

wet pussy: chibiri manko; nureman
whore: pansuke
wife: oku-san (someone else's); waifu; kanai
wonderful: suteki

young: wakai
young girl: wakai-ko